ALSO BY DIANE KEATON

Then Again
Let's Just Say It Wasn't Pretty

BROTHER & SISTER

BROTHER & SISTER

DIANE KEATON

ALFRED A. KNOPF   NEW YORK   2020

THIS IS A BORZOI BOOK
PUBLISHED BY ALFRED A. KNOPF

Copyright © 2020 by Diane Keaton

All rights reserved.
Published in the United States by Alfred A. Knopf,
a division of Penguin Random House LLC, New York,
and distributed in Canada by
Penguin Random House Canada Limited, Toronto.

www.aaknopf.com

Knopf, Borzoi Books, and the colophon are registered
trademarks of Penguin Random House LLC.

Grateful acknowledgment is made to Williamson Music Company for
permission to reprint lyric excerpt of "How Deep Is the Ocean" by
Irving Berlin © 1932 by Irving Berlin Music Company obo Williamson
Music Company. All Rights Reserved. Used With Permission.

Some names and identifying details have been
changed to protect the privacy of individuals.

Names: Keaton, Diane, author.
Title: Brother & sister / Diane Keaton.
Other titles: Brother and sister
Description: First edition. | New York: Alfred A. Knopf, 2020.
Identifiers: LCCN 2019024947 (print) | LCCN 2019024948 (ebook) |
ISBN 9780451494504 (hardcover) | ISBN 9780451494511 (epub)
Subjects: LCSH: Keaton, Diane. | Keaton, Diane—Family. | Motion
picture actors and actresses—United States—Biography.
Classification: LCC PN2287.K44 A8 2020 (print) | LCC PN2281.K44 (ebook) |
DDC 791.4302/8092 [B]—dc23
LC record available at https://lccn.loc.gov/2019024947
LC ebook record available at https://lccn.loc.gov/2019024948

Jacket photographs: (left) by Dorothy Hall; (right) by Frederic Ohringer
Jacket design by John Gall

Manufactured in the United States of America
First Edition

For Bill Clegg:

Thank you for helping me tell
"a story that was as human, and therefore as
ambivalent and as unresolved, as life itself."

—ELIA KAZAN

I'm starting to think of myself in the past tense. What I remember is what I am; a million fragments passing in a storm.

—John Randolph Hall

CONTENTS

BROTHER & SISTER

CHAPTER 1

THE PROOF IS IN THE PICTURE

The simple, sturdy, and reliable Brownie Hawkeye camera manufactured by Kodak documented our family from 1949 through 1956. Mom and Dad learned how to look into its viewfinder while selecting the right pose by pushing the button with a click. The result? Hundreds of white-framed four-inch-square pictures including my six-year-old brother Randy and eight-year-old me standing next to a clown at the Ringling Bros. and Barnum & Bailey Circus. Another shot, a year later, features all four Hall kids in the Halloween costumes Mom made. I was a Gypsy. Randy was a clown. Robin was a princess, and little Dorrie was a bunny rabbit. And there's the photograph our neighbor Ike must have taken, featuring the entire Hall family gathered on the front porch dressed in Easter Sunday outfits. Ever-ready smiles in the black-framed photographs solidified our place in history, just as the ubiquitous advertising promised. We were the stars of our very own Kodak Moments. All through these many years, Randy's smile remained a carbon copy of those that preceded it: deceptive and faraway.

In spite of our camera's all-too-ordinary results, imagery was a force to be reckoned with, especially for Mom. Thanks to her example, "looking" became a dedicated endeavor for all four of her kids. Cutting up pictures, collecting them, and making collages became a favorite form of escape and one of our primary means of expression. We weren't alone. I can't count how many times, at flea markets and antiques stores, I've come across abandoned scrapbooks packed with snapshots of long-gone families and friends on vacations, proudly displaying their new cars, holding their babies up to the lens. They were us, and we were them: another twentieth-century American family smiling into the future.

There is a photograph of Randy and me sitting at the top of a slide as a man walks our way. A young woman holds the hand of a toddler in front of a swing nearby. In the background, a power-line pole leans to the left. Behind the pole, sycamore trees stand as a barrier framing the image. Randy and I seem so undefined, so similar. Who could have known how different our lives would become, and within those differences how much would be the same.

Now, at seventy-one years of age, Randy is in the process of dying. I guess the same could be said of me, his seventy-three-year-old sister. Yet I'm the one who can still drive a car across town every weekend, sit for hours by his bed at Sunrise Villa, and watch his eyes scan the walls and ceiling until they find the window and he sets his gaze outside. I don't know how much he registers from my cheerful reports of Dorrie and Robin, or how he experiences his bedridden days. But the truth is, I've never known how Randy experienced anything. I've only heard what little he chose to say, or read what he wrote in letters or poems.

Why was his life so fraught with fear and anxiety? Even though we shared the same parents, the same schools, why were we so different? Why did he live out his life without making even one good friend? Why couldn't he stop drinking? How did he come to write with lightning-strike clarity and beauty, but also ominous violence?

For many years, when we were young, I saw Randy as an inexplicable burden. He was a nuisance, a scaredy-cat, and a crybaby. As we got older, he became an absent presence. I avoided him as my life got busier while his got smaller and more difficult.

Mother's endless need to write and record the story of The Hall Family has helped me find a path back. With her daily journal entries, and her meticulous scrapbooks filled with photographs, clippings, and letters, I've been able to see Randy from a different perspective. Even though blurry snapshots hardly tell a viable story, they do stimulate speculation. I don't know if my piecemeal version of Randy's story is true, or if I've gotten any closer to who he is and what he means to me, but I do know that I wish I could have given him more love and attention sooner. "Dear, dear, Randy," as my old friend Jean Stein would have said. Dear, dear, Randy, I do love you.

One of my favorite memories is of Randy holding Mom's hand as we ventured to downtown Los Angeles, where we saw the Christmas window displays at the Broadway Department Store. We must have been no more than four and six years old. A giant replica of Santa Claus was engulfed by better-than-ever board games, including Candyland, Go to the Head of the Class, and even The Game of Life. Stuffed animals pressed against the Madame Alexander Queen Elizabeth Dolls, who were laid out in front of the brightly lit tree. Randy screamed when he saw a Lionel train zooming around a toy village covered in what looked like real snow. The city was hopping. A couple of blocks over, Mom took us to the famous theme-driven Clifton's Cafeteria, where we picked out our favorite food and put it on our very own trays inside a giant sequoia forest as a band played on the balcony above. We were together. And Randy was happy. Mom took many photos of us as kids, but of course there is no snapshot to document my favorite outing, only a memory I can't quite trust.

John Randolph Hall was born on Sunday, March 21, 1948, at 2:13 a.m. at P. and S. Hospital in the City of Glendale, State of California. The circumference of the perfect blue-eyed, blond-haired, nineteen-inch-long baby's head measured twenty-one inches.

The first page of Mom's official Randy Scrapbook features

a large professional portrait of her one and only son. With his hair combed into a little peak at the top of his forehead, he has an unusually beguiling appeal. His eyes look off to the left, as if he's seeing something special. His tiny fist clutched into a ball touches his little mouth as if he's awestruck. Is he seeing shadows of light and dark, or the wonder of our mother's face? The baby bundled in white with a matching background of creamy perfection, this eight-by-ten-inch picture oddly mirrors a photograph I recently took of Randy at seventy. He still looks out, struck by the mystery. With those blue eyes, and his long white hair and beard, he could pass for a modern-day Moses. Two portraits. One a beginning, the other an end. One looking out, as if spellbound by a miracle. The other acknowledging a life lived on the other side of normal.

Happy greeting cards to our parents, Jack and Dorothy Hall, welcomed Baby Randy to life. "A precious little bundle tucked in a tiny bed, a world of happy plans around baby's resting head. Sincere congratulations and best of wishes too. May the world be very good to baby and to you." Signed by the Watson family, our neighbors three houses down. Several pages into the scrapbook is a very special card from Grammie Keaton that read in typical Hallmark rhyme, "You know what I just heard okay? Goodness tell me right away. Well listen here's what I was told, someone we know is two years old." Inside the envelope she included a two-dollar bill. It's still there.

More pages with more photographs gradually begin to feature Mom writing a caption below each picture as if she were Randy. "I'm three years old and the cake Grammie Hall brought was good. Our neighbors are enjoying my ice cream and cake, but it doesn't look like I'm getting any. Oh Well." "I sure do look cute in the hat mom bought at Woolworths Five and Ten Cent Store." "Here's a picture of Diane and me at the zoo looking at a monkey. I'm trying to be tough." "This is the little frog I'm holding at the Arroyo Seco stream in Pasadena." "Here I am Digging for worms on our way to Green Lake."

I don't remember a little frog at the Arroyo. I don't remember digging for worms. I don't remember Green Lake. Is there a Green Lake in Southern California? Just as I forgot we had the striped umbrella that is in the picture of Mom lying on a beach towel, shadows crossing over the back of her legs, at Huntington Beach. Were it not for the photograph of Dad, with his smiling white zinc'd face, holding the halibut he speared while skin-diving off Diver's Cove in Laguna, I wouldn't have remembered how handsome he was. I do recall his bow legs in shorts, but only because he looked like a flamingo. Years later, Grammie Hall told us it was from rickets. She chose not to go into detail. Perhaps being an abandoned single woman during the Depression had kept her uninformed of the nutritional importance of vitamin D.

Mom made sure Randy would never have to worry about rickets, but she was concerned about his fear of going outside. Perhaps the great outdoors was too expansive for him, she worried in one of her journals. But Randy was a contradiction, and eluded obvious analysis. She also noted that he loved splashing in the waves at the beach, and digging for sand crabs with his new shovel and bucket.

Underneath a photograph of a rose-covered sofa, in front of a wallpapered den, Mom, once again amusing her imaginary audience as if she were little Randy, wrote, "My first home was a Quonset Hut." This is true. For three years, until I was five or so, Randy and I shared a bedroom inside a prefabricated galvanized steel structure in the hills of Highland Park set in a cluster of trees surrounded by a community of exact replicas set in a semicircle. Just like our neighbors, we lived in a twenty-by-forty-eight-foot triangular structure with 960 square feet of usable floor space. The interior consisted of two bedrooms, a bath, kitchen, and living room. Was there a window in our bedroom? Did we see the moon at night and the sun in the morning? Was there a closet? There must have been a chest of drawers. I don't recall. The one object firmly implanted in my memory is our towering bunk bed. Every night my hands grasped the side of our ladder as my feet propelled me higher and higher, until I reached the top. In the dark, secured by my pillow, my blankie, and the quiet company of my little brother below, I was ready for sleep.

I remember glancing down from my top-bunk apartment in the sky and seeing Randy's anxious bobbing head, his fear of the dark, and his sweet if hapless face. Why was he such a chicken? Why couldn't he stop seeing ghosts that weren't there lurking in shadows? Why didn't he just drink his milk and go outside when Mom repeatedly begged him?

Somewhere around age two, Randy began calling me "Dan." As "Dan the Man," I must have enjoyed lying on my mattress in our room. Randy must have been bored with the endless details of my acquisitions. Pictured in one of Mom's Christmas photographs, there was the hand-me-down Little Homemaker Cooking Set that Auntie Martha gave me, the very special Lady Lovely Beauty Kit from Grammie Hall. But most beloved was my Betsy Wetsy Baby Doll, who could pee real water. Randy had an unusual interest in Betsy. The day he took her in his arms and buried her in the Watsons' backyard, I was so overwrought Mom forced him to go outdoors immediately, find her, and bring her back. When he returned, cradling her in his arms, she was so filthy and disheveled I threw her away. I didn't want some trashed Betsy doll.

Looking through the Randy Scrapbook, I see that Mom's Christmas and birthday letters are jam-packed with information. By three, Randy started drawing circles and talking real talk. In one of Mom's yearly birthday letters, she recounts how I took it upon myself to help teach him the way to use a pair of scissors. In the back of *McCall's* magazine, a paper doll also named Betsy became so popular they decided to include her mother, Mrs. McCall; her father, Mr. James McCall; and Nosy, a six-month-old dachshund. Betsy was my obsession. Apparently, I couldn't stop cutting out pieces of her wardrobe, including playsuits, sundresses, slacks, hoodies, and PJs. Randy must have noticed adorable little Betsy. Perhaps I helped him learn how to cut a curved line with our Crayola Safety Scissors. After all, he was my little brother, and scissors were dangerous. You could hurt yourself. These days, I wonder if pretty Betsy was a prelude to Randy's future fantasies.

Among the photographs of Randy making a sand castle, or standing under an oak tree holding my hand, or even leaning against our white picket fence in front of the Quonset hut in a ten-gallon hat, I'm reminded of the one snapshot that captures him defying the powers that be. In Grammie Hall's backyard,

Randy's holding a wastepaper basket above my head. Instead of taking it to the incinerator, he's dumping the trash on me. Perhaps Randy had caught on to the possibility that intimacy was a double-edged sword, bound together by conflict on one side and longing on the other.

In 1951, when I was five and Randy was three, Dad made a big announcement. We were going to move. He'd saved his hard-earned money and bought a house he was preparing to transport to a vacant lot on Redfield Avenue, only blocks away from all our Quonset-hut family friends. At the end of our new street was Bushnell Way Elementary School, where I would soon be attending kindergarten. We would have a lot more room to play outside. It would be fun. And since we were pretty much a family that liked to stick together, he had one more very important announcement to make. He and Mom thought we would be cheating ourselves out of much fun and happiness by not having at least one more child.

Dad's announcement was upsetting. All too soon, our little log-shaped Quonset hut would house a new family. We would no longer live in a community of unassuming, identical, heavenly homes. I must have been in a panic, because the first thing I would have worried about was our bunk bed. Surely, we could take it with us. Surely, Randy and I would continue to share our secret schemes within its safe boundaries. Surely, I'd stay in my little space at the top, vigilantly protecting Randy down below. I'd even offer to spend a few nights on the bottom bunk if we could just keep our dream world intact.

One night, after dinner, Mom and Dad sat Randy and me down for another family talk. Yet again, Dad described the new turquoise-painted home with white-trimmed windows and the big backyard. He smiled at Randy while giving him the details of the garage he'd built, and the tetherball pole he put up on the cement driveway he'd paved. Alluding to the three bedrooms in our new home, he looked at Randy and said it would be a big treat, and a lesson in independence, to have separate bedrooms. There would be no more use for a bunk bed. In a generous gesture, he decided to give it to the new Quonset hut renters, who had two children of their own. It was a gift worth giving. That's what Mom said. Or so I remember.

We didn't handle the news well. A month before we waved goodbye to our Quonset hut neighbors, Randy woke up sobbing. When Mom ran into our room, she found me sitting on the bunk-bed ladder peeing onto the floor. Randy and I didn't need more fun. We didn't want another brother or sister. We wanted to stay where we were. I continued to lobby for saving my nightly climb into a better world until the day we moved.

Looking back, I have to question whether there actually was a bunk bed. Without a four-inch-square black-and-white photograph proving its existence in either Randy's or my scrapbook, I wonder if my story of those days is a tall tale pieced together in hopes of some sort of redemption from being the bossy sister. If only Mom or Dad had taken at least one little picture to prove Randy and I really had shared such a bed. There is no such evidence, but I believe we did. I believe there was a sacred sleeping place we shared, where the dreams it encouraged overshadowed the sobering realities ahead. I can't help but think leaving our bunk bed behind to face the rigors of 440 Redfield Avenue cut short the potential for a deeper connection that might have developed as we grew older. It's hard to know, but I am certain of this: my most intimate relationship with any male took place in a pint-sized room underneath a crescent-shaped ceiling, where once upon a time I slept in a secondhand bunk bed overlooking my delicate, blond-haired brother below.

CHAPTER 2

A TOKEN OF ABSENCE

In a letter Mom typed and folded into an envelope that she placed in the Randy Scrapbook, she wrote:

Our house on 440 Redfield Avenue, Highland Park is one of the handsomest in the Valley of Hermon. Jack planted a full grown apricot tree which he dug up and moved by himself. We also planted trees in the front yard for shade. Jack constructed a tire swing for the kids to play in. I honestly don't know how he single-handedly moved a white clapboard three-bedroom bungalow to the vacant lot we now call home. Diane is a social person, always going up the hill to play with Nadine Foreman. Randy doesn't want to leave the house too much. He won't go outside unless Jack and I are working in the yard. He's afraid of airplanes. We can't tell whether it's the sound or the sight. We've taken him to the airport a few times. He loves to watch them take off and land with no fear. He can't stand it at home though. He won't tell us why. There are times I don't know how to handle Randy. He's going through a phase that's a real problem for me to know what to do. He won't let me out of his sight. He seems to suffer intensely when Jack or I get angry with him. He pleads "Don't be mad at me mom, Please."

A few months later, she wrote in her journal:

Randy is just the kind of little boy I think all boys should be. He tries so hard to please Jack. His little temper explosions are very infrequent. He still gets worked up when his toys won't behave right. But that is only impatience, and who isn't guilty of being impatient now and then. He plays by himself in the house. We had quite a mother-son talk tonight in the bathroom, I in the tub he on the toilet, so eager and anxious about his birthday, naming all the things he wants. Today was especially nice for him. Grammy Keaton came and took him shopping for whatever he wanted. He chose a big airplane which he is very proud of. He can tell you all about every detail and even take you for a ride.

I didn't like the new house. It was too big, too dark, and kind of lonely with Randy and me no longer sharing our bunk bed. He didn't seem to care one way or the other. As we gradually became more distant, I began to expand my opportunities.

I took to kindergarten and the kids my age. Our First Methodist Junior Church Choir was fun. I got to sing hymns like "This
little light of mine, I'm gonna let it shine. Let it shine, let it
shine, let it shine." Crabby old Ike, our next-door neighbor,
was not fun. He constantly complained about us kids ruining
his lawn. He hated the noise we made when Rilla Jean, a first-
grader who lived down the block, played hopscotch with me
on our concrete driveway.

While Dad continued to work as a surveyor for the Department of Water and Power, he also took classes at USC to finish
his engineering degree. What little time he had was focused on
our holidays, particularly at the beach. Mom, suddenly preg-
nant with a new baby, was elected president of the PTA, joined
the local ladies' club, and continued her churchly duties.

Robin was born in 1951. I thought for sure she must have
been adopted, because she drove me nuts from the day she
arrived. Dad seemed unusually taken with her pretty little face.
I was jealous. When she was old enough to walk and talk, she'd
snatch the French-fried potatoes off my favorite Swanson's frozen dinner. She also stole my paper cutout "Betsy McCall Has a
Merry Christmas" outfit, among other treasures.

No matter what, Randy remained the center of Mom's
attention. She fretted over his decision-making ability, his lack
of socialization, but most often his acute fear of the low-flying
planes that streaked above our home on a daily basis. Despite
these panic attacks, Randy developed a passion for the American Airlines DC-4 pressed-steel toy airplanes. None of which
made any sense, considering how he continued to come run-

ning into the house screaming for Mom at the mere sound of a DC-6 flying overhead. I used to laugh at Randy's skinny legs tripping over toys as he ran with his hands over his ears, shouting for Mom to "stop the planes." What a baby. I would count to ten after hearing the screen door slam shut; that was the amount of time it took him to reach Mom and Dad's bedroom, where he'd disappear under their bed.

In 1953, Mom's unexpected doppelgänger, little Dorrie, was born. A crybaby whose presence confirmed even less me-time with Mom, Dorrie was a pill. I'll never understand why Mom seemed so happy hauling fat-faced Dorrie around as if she were an additional appendage, helping out with baby bottles, and all the ever-changing diapers. In my opinion, Dorrie was by far the most annoying baby ever. Poor Mom. She was strapped by Robin's constant need for more toys, my jealousy, and Randy's anxiety.

Mom continued to drag us to church every weekend. No fan of God, Dad sided with us kids, for the first time. Randy dreaded getting into the Sunday-best suit Mom insisted he wear. In her journal she wrote:

Randy won't attend Sunday school unless I go and stay with him. He's three and a half and I'm still waiting to see if he will outgrow his tendency to tag after me at all times. Even at home he is at my heels. It isn't good for either of us. Last night he came into our bedroom and said "Mom, does God make the dark?" I answered yes. He said "Oh I see, so he pulls out the plug and then everything gets dark?" He's too frightened. Even on hot nights he insists I put a blanket over him "To keep the dark out."

I didn't blame Randy about the Sunday-morning ritual, which everyone hated except Mom. Hearing stories about Jesus, the son of God, flying into heaven made me wonder, where was the daughter of God? It didn't seem fair. No daughter? One day, in the middle of Sunday school, Randy ran away. Dad and a panic-stricken Mom found him sitting on the curb of busy Sherman Way Boulevard. A few months later, a brand-new upright piano was bought, a soothing device to try to make Randy happy after too much turmoil. There, seated on the bench, little Randy listened to Mom play his favorite song, Al Jolson's "Sonny Boy."

For several summers, we camped at Huntington Beach. Dad pitched our tent next to a veritable tepee city filled with other middle-class families. As soon as we stepped outside, the beach became our floor. I'd take Randy's hand and race to the shoreline to make sand castles. Dad would secure our striped umbrella while Mom fried hamburgers on the gas burner.

One memory, an idea I had, stands out: What if I was able to collect at least a couple dozen 7UP bottles and take them to the A&P grocery store, where a salesclerk would give me two cents per bottle? That way I could start saving money to buy a Mele Gold Brocade Covered Jewelry Box, including the real Gold Key. Offering to split the take, I enlisted Randy to come along and help. But he just lingered with an inexplicable grin on his face as I ransacked trash cans and searched the early-morning abandoned beach for green bottles. What was he thinking? Why didn't he want things? I figured at some point I'd do an investigation into his reasoning. It never happened. None of my bossy ways were documented in Mom's Randy Scrapbook, yet we did search for 7UP bottles near the old salt-water plunge in Huntington Beach. And I did walk away with six dollars and fifty cents. I have to confess I didn't share the money I made, but of course, Randy never asked.

My happiest early memories of being Randy's big sister were at the beach, in the waves, making sand castles and acting out fantasy stories based on *The Wizard of Oz*. Randy never took the lead role in any of our scenes, but I remember him taking it all very seriously. I also remember how much Randy loved our walks to the pier. Mom would carry a bag of bread crumbs as Dad held little Dorrie in his arms. Robin, Randy, and I fed the seagulls. Randy was enchanted by the big bird's ability to catch bread in its mouth midair. He was convinced they did it in slow motion. With their big webbed feet and their giant-sized wings, seagulls were his idea of magic.

The bonds we once shared in our bunk-bed days were thinning. But Randy stayed loyal to me. He didn't, for example, rat me out on the day I pushed him off a dirt hill and onto an old sycamore log, where he broke his leg. He told Mom it was an accident. It was the same year I voted myself in as president of the Beaver's Club, a secret society whose sole mission was the acquisition of pelts, particularly rabbit's feet. I reminded myself that being self-elected to supervise its six members was a huge responsibility, so I informed Randy I'd chosen Rilla Jean Williams as vice-president, over him. After all, she had access to her grandfather's seven rabbit's-foot key chains. Randy didn't seem to care. He agreed it was important to make Rilla Jean happy. What a pushover. It was just like the 7UP bottle money. He didn't care. He just didn't care.

On a hazy summer day in 1956, Dad took a photograph of eight-year-old Randy, thirty-five-year-old Mom, and ten-year-old me at the Zzyzx desert resort, tucked away in San Bernardino County. In the foreground we form a triangle in the swimming pool. A wind barrier cuts the Soda Mountains in half. My body is turned away as I begin to lift myself out of the water. At the edge of the pool, Randy stands on tiptoes. He leans forward with his arms outstretched as he reaches for Mom, who's wearing a fetching black swimsuit with a white bathing cap. As I study the four-by-four-inch black-and-white snapshot, I see Mom's wide-open fingers waiting in anticipation. I also take note of Randy's head. Was it always so large?

A series of haphazard memories comes rushing in. Mom and her friend Willie Blandon, my Dad's friend Bob's wife, watching us kids play in the waves at Diver's Cove Beach in Laguna. I remember overhearing them share a private conversation on the subject of giving birth. When Randy's name came up, they used a series of unusual words to explain something I didn't understand. "Forceps" was repeated several times. What did that mean? A few years later, we were eating lunch when Mom, once again with Willie, spoke of a friend who'd lost her first baby while giving birth. As they elaborated on the difficulty some infants have coming down the birth canal, Randy's name was once again brought up, along with words like "cervix" and "forceps." More puzzled than ever, I wondered what they meant.

Twenty-five years later, lying on a couch and looking at my analyst Dr. Landau's white plastered ceiling in New York City, I listened to her describe forceps as having the appearance of large salad spoons with pincers. Sometimes they were used to assist babies with heads too large for the mother's pelvis as they came down the birth canal. If pulled too hard, some infants had lasting psychological issues. She described learning difficulties in children that could be traced back to birth patterns, which included issues relating to stress, decision making, and, for some, even the inability to initiate and complete projects. As she went on, I kept thinking of all the assumptions I'd made about Randy and his so-called Problems. Had he been the victim of a botched medical procedure pulling him into life? I never had the courage to question Mom. I never asked her if Randy's had been a difficult birth. I never asked her what it was like for her to have a son like Randy. I must have been afraid of her responses. I didn't want to know her sadness. I didn't want to know anything about these parts of my mother's life. Not only back then, but for a long time after. Now, as life would have it, I study her journals and scrapbooks, photographs and letters, still looking for clues.

In the photograph of the three of us at the Zzyzx desert resort, I look at the distance between Randy's outstretched arms and my mother's waiting hands. When Dad clicked the camera before the instant Randy leapt, he must have been caught off guard by Mud's beauty (Mud's what he used to call Mom when he was smitten). Maybe he wanted to capture her allure forever and ever. Maybe Dad, like Randy, needed a mother to take care of him too. I doubt he could have foreseen the enormity of the challenges that were yet to come. Mom did, though. Mom knew.

After she died in 2008, I became the family documentarian. Suddenly I was in possession of her thirty-two journals, fifteen family scrapbooks, twenty photo albums, hundreds of letters, plus Dad's yearbook from USC, and his brochures for Hall and Foreman Inc. Later, when Randy could no longer take care of his things, I became the sole possessor of his two published poetry books, five hundred collages, fifty-four notebooks, and seventy random journals filled with his own brand of cartoons—including my brother's entire collection of the intimate feelings, fantasies, and disappointments underlying the mystery of his life. I want to understand that mystery. Or at least try to understand the complexity of loving someone so different, so alone, and so hard to place. I wanted to write Randy's story, and my story of being his sister, because there are so many people who live through the sorrow and pain of not knowing how to manage a family member who has a singularly unique view of life: a sibling who doesn't fit in or follow the paths the rest of us take; who challenges and bewilders, upsets and dazzles us; who scares some of us away; but who still loves us, in his or her way.

CHAPTER 3

KING OF THE BACK FLIP

At the end of 1956, all six Hall family members piled into the station wagon and hopped onto Interstate 5, leaving our turquoise-blue house behind. Dad had applied for and got the job of Assistant Director of Public Works in Santa Ana. It was a big step up, with a significantly larger salary. On our way to the brand-new four-bedroom tract house, Randy wanted to know how long it would take to get there. Mom replied, "Sooner than you think, honey, sooner than you think." Dad chimed in with "It's a thirty-mile drive." That seemed like a long way to go for a new home. I was ten, Randy eight, Robin six, and Dorrie three.

Our beige house at 905 North Wright Street seemed like an example of what magazines described then as middle-class modern living at its best. After our first few months, Mom wrote a letter, which I found in her Santa Ana family scrapbook:

Not wanting to sound like a candidate for the great American family, I must say these are happy days for us here in Santa Ana. Of course, it's all due to Jack. I can't put into words what a good husband he is, but I'll let it go at that. His work is very hard. He seems to like it though. It's done much to improve him for the world of public relations. As first assistant city Engineer not only does he maintain roads, bridges, and buildings he also helps with management skills and budgetary requirements. He's very busy taking management classes on Tuesday night, Toastmasters on Wednesday night and usually Friday for the engineer's meeting. On Saturdays, he tries to go to Indian Scouts with Randy. Jack and I are surely blessed by God. We are so thankful. Our children are a great joy to us. Randy, with his depth of feeling and sensitivity which I constantly pray to God we don't ruin. Someday in some way he'll be able to give and let out this ability he has to sense beauty and fine things. But most important of all is Daddy, and husband Jack, who has an uncanny knowledge of what's right and wrong. He is the main reason we are such a close family. Daddy is definitely the head and we all know it, and like it. I haven't words to put down my feelings for Jack. He's part of me, that's all, and that's the best part.

In the new house we ate our meals at the beige tiled bar separating the kitchen from the dining room. Mom, seated on a stool near the stove, sat opposite the rest of us. Dad hunkered in near the window overlooking our neighbors Maxine and Joe's identical home across the street. We kids didn't have a designated spot. The Bastendorfs, our next-door neighbors to the right, had a jungle filled with desert plants for a lawn. We'd never seen anything like it. Laurel Bastendorf introduced Mom to the trendy 1950s-modern *Sunset* magazine. We were enthralled by her beatnik manner. Mr. Rohrs and his wife, our other neighbors, lived on the corner. Marie, their daughter, was painfully shy. We steered clear of Mr. Rohrs, who was a tough-minded high-school principal.

Every night, after dinner, Randy begged Mom to let him watch *The Bullwinkle Show*. Each episode began with Rocky, a flying squirrel, soaring over a snow-covered mountain. His companion Bullwinkle, a lovable moose, was, in my opinion, an idiot. Randy would endlessly repeat their lame jokes. "How about this one, you guys? So Rocky looks at Bullwinkle and says, 'If you want to inherit a fortune you have to spend a weekend at the Abominable Manor.' Bullwinkle says, 'That's no problem. I've been living in an abominable manner all my life.'"

Only Mom laughed, which of course encouraged Randy to try another. "Listen to this one, Dan."

"My name is not Dan," I would tell him.

"Okay, Dan. This is a good one. You're going to like it. You know the evil Boris Badenov, right?"

"Right."

"Okay. So Boris shakes his head at Natasha Fatale saying, 'Ah, it's good to be back on campus!' She says, 'Boris, you went to college? Where? Penn State?' He shakes his head: 'No, State Pen!!!' Get it?"

Dad didn't get it and didn't want to. But Mom, Randy's greatest audience, cheered him on.

Four bedrooms was a big step up from three. Robin and Dorrie's faced the roofed-in patio across from me. Mine looked onto the driveway, where Dad parked his Santa Ana City loaner car, one of the perks of his prestigious new position. With such a unique gift, we were suddenly elevated into a two-car family. On my desk, I displayed my very own hardback copy of *The Diary of Anne Frank,* the first book that made me cry. With time, I saved enough money to buy two travel posters from France, where, I decided, I was going to go as soon as I graduated from high school. Randy's bedroom was at the end of the long hallway next to the kids' bathroom, and across from Mom and Dad's master suite. Besides a bed, Randy's den of hibernation had a long table, where his collection of junk rapidly grew, beneath a window that seemed to offer no light. With time, his room became a haphazard mess, housing ugly plastic dinosaurs surrounded by stacks of horror comics and *Mad* magazines with weird-looking gap-toothed Alfred E. Neuman on the cover.

It was a rare occasion when one of us ventured into Mom and Dad's bedroom and private bath. In a way it seemed like an off-limits, separate home of its own. We didn't knock on their door. Once in a while, I felt sorry that Randy's room was not only next to the ever-populated family bathroom, but also across the hall from the mystery of Mom and Dad's suite.

Through the doors, he must have been privy to their slowly evolving relationship.

As often as possible, Randy retreated to his bedroom. It was there that his preteen fantasies took form. I knew because Rocky Lee, his friend from up the block, took me aside one day and told me that Randy, who was thirteen, had found a *Playboy* magazine near the Rohrses' orange grove and hidden it under his bed. Being a good Christian, I sneaked in, grabbed the *Playboy,* and ran down the hall screaming for Mom. After all, wasn't sex a sin in God's eyes? With Jesus Christ and his father, God, on my side, I conveniently erased the fact that Randy had never ratted me out.

As Randy's fantasies secretly grew behind his bedroom door, Mom was busy spiffing up our new home. She took particular pride in decorating the mostly unused living room with homemade shell boards, a mosaic coffee table, and a framed print of a Maurice de Vlaminck landscape. *Sunset* magazines were laid on top of the coffee table in front of the modern couch, with two upholstered chairs on either side. On occasion, Mom would make popcorn and we'd all gather there as Dad projected our color slides. One image has withstood the test of time: Randy, standing on our brand-new Griswold-Nissen trampoline, three and a half feet off the ground, is smiling with unexpected authenticity. There is no blank-faced grin. His blond hair is short. His ears stick out like two small buttons. He's wearing a white tee shirt and a pair of blue shorts that highlight a set of great-looking long legs. Contrary to my memory of a weak, unexceptional boy, Randy is handsome. But most of all, he's self-assured. Standing on the trampoline, framed against a gray sky with me behind him, Randy is a study in confident, spontaneous joy.

Looking at this slide now, I'd lay ten-to-one odds he'd just completed a perfect backward flip. Why else are his arms flexed as if he were Superman? It's not that Robin and Dorrie couldn't perform their own stunts; it's that Randy was the master of both the forward and backward flip. He wasn't afraid of upside down. Maybe engaging in an out-of-sync world gave him a sense of power, even authority. He didn't mind letting his body say goodbye to gravity.

As King of the Back Flip, Randy let go of everyday constraints. He must have had a plethora of eureka moments on that old Griswold-Nissen, but he never talked about them, nor did he boast of his dexterity. He was not a braggart. He chose to explore wrong-side-up thoughts in secret. I can imagine Mom's disappointment when the click of the camera didn't capture Randy spinning in midair. Perhaps she felt hemmed in by Dad's mandates: "Don't get carried away with lassoing dreams, Dot."

That was around the time he nicknamed her "Dot." Maybe it was inspired by Frank Sinatra's rendition of "Polka Dots and Moonbeams": "I learned the meaning of the words 'Ever after' / And I'll always see polka dots and moonbeams." Sometimes I wonder if he was jealous of her singular affection for Randy. I can imagine him laying down the law, telling her not to waste what little money she had in her budget by taking too many pictures of a son who needed structure.

For Dad, it was always about money, just as it had been with his mother. Grammie Hall was tight with a buck. Not only was she a fairly successful neighborhood loan shark, who hid money under the floor in her closet; she didn't trust anyone, including her son. Somewhere in Mom's old journals, I found a highly unusual letter from Dad to Grammie Hall dated June 11, 1960.

Hi Ma.
Well, Dorothy and I didn't do too good in Las Vegas.
I want to thank you for buying our meals and paying
for the rooms. It made the trip very inexpensive. I am
attaching the last payment on my loan from you. The
amount borrowed was $7904.45 at 3 percent interest.
This was a very good deal for me. Thanks. I made 185
payments to you of 100 dollars each. I never missed
a payment once. If you have any questions. Let me
know.
    Love, Jack

Poor Dad. After he passed away, I remember going through a chest of drawers where I found several Gerber jars full of pennies, nickels, and dimes invading the socks. Quarters and fifty-cent pieces were saved in red-and-white-striped paper rolls the bank passed out to its loyal customers. Dad oversaw the saving of his hard-earned money with caution, care, and concern. And he chose to make sure every investment he made on behalf of the family was thrifty, almost to the point of causing a different kind of risk.

The letter to Grammie Hall, along with cutting back on Mom's thirty-seventh birthday by presenting her with a box of See's candy and a five-dollar bill, may have been a result of his "new idea." Dad was determined to create his own engineering firm. He began to map out a plan, but, more important, cut back on family fun time to save money. There would be no pitched tent at Huntington Beach, and certainly no trips to Disneyland in 1958. Tucking us in at night, Mom would tell us Dad was wrestling with big ideas that would, she said, "change our lives for the better." But it wasn't clear to me what "better" meant. For Randy, stuck between Mom's unvocalized demands to try harder, and Dad's so-called helping out with homework, it was all too much. Sometimes I could hear Dad harping behind Randy's shut door: "For God's sake, think it through." Or "I just told you, four times six is twenty-four. Got it? Add six four times and memorize the damn thing." "Damn" and even an occasional "goddamn" became frequent additions to his vocabulary. He disappeared into longer workdays, and at home he'd stopped utilizing the soft sell with us the kids, and with Mom, too, in favor of the hard.

For all of Dad's successfully executed plans, he didn't have a methodology to solve the mystery of his blond-haired boy. I don't know if Randy recoiled from Dad, or from his drive. I can't imagine what it was like for him to be Jack Hall's disappointment. "Pick up your junk." "What are you doing? That's not the way to mow a lawn. At least finish the damn job, *son*!!!" Dad's struggles further fueled his impatience with all his children, but especially Randy. Following a host of mandated masculine endeavors such as Toastmasters, Boy Scouts, and skin-diving off the Palos Verdes cliffs with Dad's friend Bob Blandon and his son Gary didn't help. Even though Randy reluctantly learned how to string a bow for Indian Scouts, cut abalone meat from its shell, and on occasion catch a fly ball in Little League, he knew he would never become what our father wanted him to be.

Dad's ambition, his work ethic, his awkward relationship with his son, his disappointment, his longing to help Randy even though he didn't know how, were beginning to look like failure—Dad's least favorite word. Randy had no interest in becoming Jack Hall, Jr. In his journal, he would later write:

> I didn't think much of my father. Every time he came home I was scared the whole night, which means every night. My youth was full of seagulls circling the beach, and a freedom that only came to me when I saw waves burst from the rocks or smelled salt on my sunburned skin. Now my eyes are full of saltwater. Dad left me long ago.

CHAPTER 4

A HAWK'S TALONS

In 1960, thirty-nine-year-old Jack Hall quit his job at Santa Ana City Hall to become the president of Hall and Foreman Inc. Mom wrote:

> It was a risky choice, but Jack held firm with a kind of courage that surprised everyone. He must be given 100 percent credit for his business acumen by applying his mentor Dale Carnegie's tried and true techniques. I'm sure we will all look back and remember when dad took off on his own and never stopped. I'm writing it all down so we will have evidence to make it clear that on June 18th he left the city of Santa Ana to start Hall and Foreman.

Dad was smart to partner with his former boss, Hugh Foreman. Their detailed résumé specified a responsibility for overseeing civil engineering, environmental planning, and land surveying on everything from housing developments to office buildings. As a mid-century modern businessman, not only was Dad a charming salesman, but he was, as the saying goes, honest to a fault. He didn't take his cue from Grammie Hall, the former neighborhood loan shark. Oh no, he had a grander vision of what all his planning, self-improvement, and hard work would deliver, and it did.

I doubt any family member, including Mom, understood what engineering really meant. According to Wikipedia, "Civil engineers survey installations, establish reference points, and guide construction. They estimate the quantities and cost of materials and equipment." In other words, he designed and created sound civil structures, "a series of connected elements that form a system which can resist a series of external load effects applied to it." He worked hard on public projects like highway improvements and bridge construction, sidewalks, and parking lots.

At home, Dad seemed frustrated. Apparently, the principles of his day job didn't apply to fatherhood. Still, he urged us to "Plan Ahead" and "Be Positive." He even tried to teach us how to have firm handshakes. God only knew what he was going to do with his four drifty children. Every day he methodically built his business, ascending both professionally and financially. And every night he came home to us, where we presented him with our stubborn fragility.

After just a few years on Wright Street, Mom began to understand she was on a one-way street, heading into a future filled with more of the same. There was no going back to dreams she didn't have the courage to admit she wanted. Not only was she the mother of four children; she was also playing the role of mother to a man whose own mother hadn't been mother material. As Dorothy's husband, Jack felt entitled to her undivided attention. When he complained about clients who wouldn't pay their bills on time, she'd reassure him: "Don't worry, honey. Keep at it. Don't let it affect your mood. It's time Hugh Foreman stepped up and supported your efforts with more zeal!" She single-handedly gave him enough confidence to think through psychologically complex issues, which in turn helped sustain the firm's success.

When it became all too apparent no one was going to encourage her own dreams, Mom's world darkened. After a while, Jack Hall couldn't help but perceive Dorothy as yet another employee, one whose job included the distribution of three meals a day, shopping, decorating, washing, researching extracurricular activities for the kids, and, yes, if time permitted, the pursuit of her artistic hobbies. But only if. After all, he was paying for everything, including her shiny new Buick station wagon.

In response, Mom may have unconsciously pitted us against Dad. The driving force of her unspoken resentment was his attempt to turn Randy into his kind of man. Her solution was to form a secret society in which the four of us kids unwittingly excluded our father. When he unexpectedly came home during one of Mom's after-school fun sessions over crackers and cheddar cheese, his presence meant that fun took a back seat. He wasn't welcome.

In her journal, she kept close tabs on twelve-year-old Randy's progress at Willard Junior High School, especially his potential gift in writing.

Willard seems to be the school Randy needed. All the movement from class to class, the feeling of adulthood; he even buys his own lunch now. Apparently, there's no trouble with the locker set up and he brings his schoolwork home every night. I see a new boy in the making. One week has gone by and suddenly he's eager to get to the bus at 7 am. He even prepared a paper on "Safeguarding our American Freedom." We went to the library for books and ideas and made it home in time to battle out a theme before dinner. The result: his paper was one of the 15 chosen for final judging. He was very pleased with the outcome. He's such a good kid. One needs to spark him up a bit. He has no trouble sparking when he's interested in something.

I can't remember Randy's presence at any of my landmark moments at Willard. When I was elected class secretary, and when I finally became a Melodette Songbird and performed for local groups such as the Kiwanis Club or the PTA's annual Founders Day Luncheon, he showed no interest. But, then, why would he? After I sang "All I Want for Christmas Is My Two Front Teeth" for Willard's talent show, Randy didn't seem to notice, but I didn't have time to monitor his accomplishments, either. Still, it was odd. I never saw him hanging out with friends. He didn't seem to have any.

One weekend afternoon, when I was sixteen and Randy was fourteen, I heard noises coming from down the hallway as I was cutting out pictures from *Mademoiselle* magazine's special issue for "The Girl Moving Up."

Someone was screaming. Running toward Randy's room, I heard Mom shout the word "divorce" as Dad yelled back, "Jesus Christ, get one."

When I opened Randy's door, I found him sitting at his desk, reading *Mad* magazine as if nothing were happening. The yelling got louder. "What's going on?" I whispered. "Oh my God, do you think they're going to get a divorce? I'm scared." My heart was pounding. I asked him if we should call the police. Tears started rolling down my face. Without so much as a glance my way, Randy put the magazine down, got up, opened the door, and then started running down the hall toward the front door. I tried to stop him. "Randy, what's going to happen? Shouldn't we do something?" As he reached the front door, I grabbed him, looked into his eyes, and begged him to go back and try to talk to them. Couldn't he hear them throwing things? They might hurt each other. Without so much as a nod, Randy slipped out of my grip and ran outside. He never bothered to look back.

Hours later, when he did return, it was as if the incident had never happened. There was the seemingly usual dinner that night, and the nights thereafter. When I tried to talk to Randy, he just shrugged his shoulders and walked off. Gradually, Mom and Dad's arguments became more frequent, but also harder to detect. From behind the bedroom door at the end of the narrow hallway, their anger pushed Randy deeper into an even more solitary world, where normalcy was no longer an expectation.

Not long after I left for New York to study acting at the Neighborhood Playhouse School of the Theatre, Mom and Dad moved the family to a new, more expensive house on Towner Street.

Dorrie wrote me about how Randy was faring:

Dear Diane,
Randy has a few hippie friends. He wears high boots tucked into his pants with a suede jacket. His hair is kind of a Beatle cut brushed to one side. He looks very handsome and put together. He plays the guitar and writes, even sings songs. Here's one. It goes like this: "I am a freak at the fair, people stare but I don't care, I am a freak at the fair." We haven't told dad about his view that working to obtain material things and prestige stand in the way of more meaningful pursuits. For Randy meaningful pursuits means writing poetry. He uses unusual imagery, and strange thoughts of a random, even confessional nature.
      Love, Dorrie

In June 1966, Randy graduated from high school. I flew home from New York City to attend the ceremony and stay for the summer. As he walked to the podium to accept his diploma, he looked pretty dandy in his cap and gown. Mom and Dad were beaming. After all, Randy had succeeded in continually getting up at 6:30 a.m. each school day to trudge his way to and from classrooms for three years. Wasn't that what high school was all about? As we sat in the grandstand of the same high-school auditorium where I'd graduated two years before, Dad looked at Mom with a combination of pride and willed optimism and said, "That boy is a sleeper, and someday . . . watch out."

My summer vacation in the new three-thousand-square-foot home on North Towner Street revealed an underlying sadness in everyone, even though our family had entered the upper middle class by purchasing a house for the exorbitant price of forty thousand dollars. It was a big step up from Wright Street, to a much more upscale Santa Ana neighborhood. The backyard was dominated by an oversized pool with a little fountain in the middle. The unattached former maid's room became Randy's private bedroom. With a new stereo setup, he introduced Dorrie and Robin to Frank Zappa, Bob Dylan, Joan Baez, and Joni Mitchell. I slept in what felt like guest accommodations. Remnants from my past had all but disappeared. We'd rarely pile into the station wagon and drive to the beach; camping was a thing of the past. Dad didn't have time to surf with his old buddy Bob Blandon. On the plus side, Robin and Dorrie no longer had to share a bedroom. Mom was busy working on her teaching degree at Cal State Fullerton. Hall and Foreman was a flourishing enterprise. Our dinners were eaten in an actual dining room. Along with serving the meal, Mom placed a new bottle of wine on the table every night. My days were spent bleaching my hair blond, shopping with Mom when she had time, hanging out with Dorrie and Robin, and occasionally visiting Randy's world.

After a couple of months, I noticed that Dad was even more dependent than before on Mom's approval, as well as on her limitless interest in encouraging his pursuits. With more adult eyes, I could see that, in a way, he was just another one of us kids. He'd ask her advice on how to deal with clients who wouldn't pay the bills, or how to handle lazy employees. She alone helped propel him into a more profitable career. When September approached, and I was heading back to begin my second year at the Neighborhood Playhouse, I wondered if any one of us would ever encourage Mom's dreams.

Later that year, one of Robin's letters began by describing a loss of innocence in America, a sort of national feeling of anger. She wrote about the Vietnam War, and all the young men who were dying for our country. Nobody talked about it at home. She was worried Randy might be drafted.

Randy does hang out with an occasional friend now and then. With them he laughs and appears incredibly easy to be around. The Randy I see on these occasions strikes me as more like a façade. But then putting on a façade is something everyone in our family is good at. This may sound strange, but sometimes I wonder if he might be someone I wouldn't want to know. Mom's the one who's most touched by him. To me he doesn't fit the description of a brother. It's hard to understand him. I really don't think anybody does, not even mom. His room is sort of barren looking.

On the plus side, I wish you could have seen mom's surprise when he got a A in his creative writing class at Santa Ana Junior College. Apparently, his teacher told him his poetry was interesting, so much so she's going to submit one to the school paper. Mom was beaming when she told me, "He will make it, just you wait and see, he will make it."

Miss you,
Love Rob

And then, later that same year, this letter from Mom:

Dear Diane,
Randy got a notice to report to the Draft. He needs a doctor's letter stating that he's unable to fight in a war. It's a disturbing element in all our lives. Last week he went for the physical and got sick, so I had to pick him up. Tomorrow he goes back. Grandma Hall called to see what happened. She thinks he was scared! Well, why not? Wouldn't you be? What does everyone have against peace? A letter arrived the other day asking for verification from a psychologist that Randy's unable to serve. It felt like a threat. He's so anxious!

Love, mom

Mom made Randy see a psychiatrist, who sent a letter to the draft board assuring the powers that be that a certain John Randolph Hall from Santa Ana, California, was not fit to serve. I wonder now what Mom did with that letter, and, moreover, what it said about Randy's psychological problems. According to Dorrie, Dad did not discuss Randy's Conscientious Objection to the war, or the so-called medical issue that got him out of induction. Vietnam was no longer a topic of conversation over dinner. Instead, Dad began pushing Randy to come work at Hall and Foreman. Randy responded with that goofy "okey-dokey" manner, as if everything was all right, even though it wasn't. Most of the time he'd stay in his room and wouldn't come out. To Dorrie, the whole draft event was strange, because Randy previously appeared to have every intention of enlisting. She wondered if there was a disconnect between how Randy presented himself and who he was.

At the Neighborhood Playhouse, I was consumed with envy. Cricket Cohen got all of chain-smoking guru Sandy Meisner's praise. I was having a hard time "living truthfully under given imaginary circumstances."

One day, in the middle of a repetition exercise that began with an observation, I said, "Cricket, why are you smiling at me?"

Cricket responded with "I'm not smiling at you. You look jealous of my power," or something like that, anyway.

I replied, "You're not smiling at me?"

Cricket said, "Why would I waste my time responding to such a dumb remark?"

"A dumb remark?" I said.

Suddenly Mr. Meisner stopped the exercise, pointed his finger in my face, and said, "There's a slight chance you're going to be a good actress someday. But you desperately need to experience more life and stop being so damn general," which was another way of saying I hadn't taken notice of Cricket's attitude, nor did I seem bold enough to follow my instincts instead of repeating such half-assed responses.

Twice a month, I'd walk down the stairs of the Rehearsal Club, a theatrical girls' boarding house and my home away from home, and dutifully put quarters into the pay phone attached to the basement wall. I'd listen to family news. Robin had a new boyfriend, named Bob Gulley. Mom was almost finished with her college degree. Dad's business was doing well. Dorrie got straight A's on her report card. I did not ask about Randy's state of mind.

One day, a large manila envelope was waiting for me at the front desk. Inside, Mom had sent a recent photograph taken with her new Nikon F camera. The back of the eight-by-ten-inch black-and-white picture was stamped "Dorothy Hall 845 North Towner Street, Santa Ana, California 91706 Photographer." On the front, Randy's nineteen-year-old hand leans against a thin wooden railing. A hawk's talons are wrapped around its circumference. With its back to the camera, the hawk outstretches its wings, as if ready to fly into the background of a hazy, endless sky.

Looking back at this picture, taken fifty years ago, I now see a hawk about to airlift his next meal, my brother's extended hand. On Randy's middle finger, I recognize one of the six silver rings Mother made for each family member the summer she took a silversmith workshop at Santa Ana Junior College. Each ring was an emblem of her endless pursuit of love. Who but our mother would make six identical rings, one for each of us, in honor of securing our eternal bond?

I imagine Randy admiring the hawk, especially its visual acuity. I can picture him trying to understand the hawk's perfectly timed sudden dashes from hidden perches, to sink its talons into some unlucky lizard or frog. Randy must have loved speculating on the hunt and its consequences. I doubt that Randy took into consideration that a hawk might be free from pondering the full cycle of its actions.

Even though Mom's photograph reveals nothing more than a wooden railing, a faceless hawk flapping its wings, a silver band on an unusually long-fingered hand in the middle of a white background, it tells a story. In one of his journals, Randy writes: "In an old photograph, I'm looking in the wrong direction. Even now I watch out the wrong window for a falling star. But, once again it is somebody else's miracle."

Miracles were scarce back at home. Robin and Dorrie both reported that drinking had become a nightly ritual with our parents. Even before Mom's glass was half empty, Dad would insist on refilling it. According to Robin, Mom was struggling with change. I was long gone. Randy retreated to his room as often as possible. One night, she told me, our parents had a huge fight over the fact that I didn't want to go on family vacation that summer. Mom, as expected, stuck up for me. After a lot of yelling, Dad suddenly got out of control and threw a wine bottle at her. It smashed against the kitchen wall. This was the beginning of a separation that lasted almost six months.

Mom did not include this episode in her journal. No longer part of the daily family dynamic, I felt sad but also confused about my parents' relationship, and the effect it must be having on Robin and Dorrie, and of course Randy. Mom moved to the little cabin in Silverado Canyon, north of Santa Ana, they'd bought a few years before. She took Robin and Dorrie with her. To this day, I'll never understand why she tried to talk Randy into staying with Dad. But he wasn't having it . . . not at all. Jack Hall was destined to live alone in the sprawling home two blocks north of 17th Street in Santa Ana.

Even though my decision had triggered the fight, Randy remained the focus of our family's conflicts. Dad, never welcomed in Mom's exclusive inner circle, was now defective material. Yet in all her journals she continued to insist that life, for the most part, was a breeze. "An interesting comment today from a shopkeeper. He mentioned he was buying for Christmas now!! Can you believe in late May? Talk about commercial trickery." "Off to Elfin forest in Escondido mountains; lots of hiking trails." "Robin loves the nursing classes she's taking. It's so good to see her feel so confident and proud." "Had a long talk with Dorrie about college." "Randy's taken to playing one of his three guitars all over the house. He has to become great. He loves Music like a deep all consuming gift." That was Mom.

After emotions had cooled, she moved back to her apologetic Jack. At this point, Randy, in an effort to clear things up with Dad, and no doubt encouraged by Mom, told Dad he was having a hard time deciding what to do with his life. He said he felt he needed more of an education and talked about enrolling at Santa Ana Junior College full time. Dad liked the initiative and offered him a part-time job at Hall and Foreman. Randy took it.

B ack home, in a journal entry from 1968, Mom wrote:

I'm so excited Randy's taking a few classes at Santa
Ana. He's also working part time at Hall and Foreman learning how to be a surveyor. We decided to let
him stay in the Silverado Canyon Cabin. He loves his
independence. He met a young woman named Sally
Tharpe at work. Her father is a judge in San Diego.
It's all very vague. I don't exactly know what Sally's
job is in the office, but she seems nice. They've dated
a few times. I'm very excited for him. Randy's never
had a girlfriend before. Sally has a son from a previ-
ous marriage, a boy named Johnny. This is all new
territory.

Randy never mentioned Sally to me. On the other hand,
how could he have? We didn't talk then, nor did we corre-
spond. One time, he reached out by sending me a few of his
poems: "Diane. Take a look and see what you think. Thanks a
bunch. Love Randy." There, among several pieces with titles
like "China Paint" and "Passing Over," I read a passage that
stuck.

*The yellow tongue of the calla lily draws a hummingbird to
its bell-shaped mouth. The hummer hangs in the morning air
before plunging its head into the velvet hollow. Her well is dry.
In the twitch of a particle what "is" becomes what "was."*

Randy liked the quiet atmosphere of Silverado Canyon. He continued working for Dad, which was made bearable with Sally in the office. Their relationship grew. She kept Randy grounded. Soon enough, she moved in with him. Mom surmised he was genuinely in love, although, as was typical of Randy, he chose not to share his feelings.

I remember meeting Sally for the first time on a surprise trip I made home that Easter. In their free time, Randy and Robin had been working on a singing act. He wrote the music and played the guitar, while Robin performed the vocals. On Wednesday nights, one of the local clubs let prospective performers try out their songs on an audience. Mom and I drove up to sit at the bar with Sally and watch them sing. At ten-thirty, after a long set by one of the regulars, the owner introduced Randy and Robin. Randy was pretty drunk. As Robin began to sing, I was surprised by her sweet, lilting voice, and by how beautiful she looked onstage. Watching Randy was almost unbearable. He seemed so vulnerable, his feelings were so transparent, I thought he might cry. At the end of their brief set, he asked the manager if there was time to sing another song. Greeted with "Not now," Randy walked out of the bar. Sally followed. I'd never seen Randy ask for anything.

Later, we found them outside the cabin, sharing a pint of beer. After the experience at the club, he never did ask for anything, with the exception of asking Sally for her hand in marriage.

CHAPTER 5

TILL DEATH DO US PART

Not long after I graduated from the Neighborhood Play-house, I was cast in the Broadway musical *Hair*. Since I was not a hippie, or much of a singer, I was stunned. For eight months of 1968, I was a tribe member who sang in a trio, "Black Boys." I remember lying under a huge scrim, night after night, watching a variety of tribe members stand up naked as Claude, played by James Rado, sang "Where Do I Go?" The music was great, and the play had a dizzy energy audiences loved. Still, I wondered where *I* was going, and what would come next.

What came next was more than I ever could have imag-ined. When I landed an audition for Woody Allen's *Play It Again, Sam,* on Broadway, miracle of miracles, I got the female lead. Woody was brilliant, hilarious, and cute, too. In *Lovers and Other Strangers,* my first movie, I was cast in a small part, a young woman in the middle of a divorce. The year was 1970. At my audition for *The Godfather,* I thought it was a waste of time. I was not the kind of actress to play a fine upper-class young woman happy to marry and take a back seat to the likes of Michael Corleone. What were they thinking? I didn't even want the part.

Life started flying by. I rarely went home to California, nor did I focus on what was going on there. I knew Randy had continued to share Mom and Dad's little getaway cabin in Silverado Canyon with Sally. I didn't bother to ask Randy how things were going. In May 1973, having finished my fourth movie, Woody Allen's *Sleeper,* I had enough money to rent a nice brownstone apartment on the Upper West Side. I was firmly planted in New York City, and my acting life had taken a definite turn for the better. One day, I got a call from Mom. She had an announcement to make: Randy was getting married.

Two months later, on the morning of July 21, 1973, I was home with the family, getting ready for the wedding that would take place later that day behind the cabin in Silverado Canyon. Grammie Hall called, wanting to know if I thought it would be all right for her to wear the new pantsuit she'd bought at the Ivers department store. She was bringing George Olsen, our stand-in grandfather and Grammie's longtime tenant/companion of thirty years, who did magic tricks with cards, and fed pigeons little pieces of old bread out of his hand. Before Grammie hung up, she wanted to tell me something important: "A good marriage can be a turning point, Diane, and a turning point is just what Randy needs. Before Sally, he was turning into a do-nothing bum!"

At four o'clock in the afternoon, thirty-five people were drinking sangria under the eucalyptus trees, waiting for Sally's father, Judge Ross Tharpe, to begin the ceremony. Mrs. Tharpe, Sally's mother, was a formidable figure in her bright-yellow dress. As Randy walked down the aisle with a new haircut in an embroidered white wedding shirt, wearing a big grin, Robin, Dorrie, Mom, Dad, and I were nothing short of amazed. I'd never seen Randy look like that; he'd literally been transformed by the occasion. When the "Wedding March" began to play, Sally, in a Mexican-themed white brocaded dress, with her strawberry-blond hair tied back, seemed to float toward her destiny, looking attractive, and strong. She had a bold presence.

Judge Tharpe wore the traditional black robe, with prayer book in hand. As Sally and Randy vowed to stick it out "through sickness and health . . . till death do us part," Randy placed the ring on Sally's finger. Mother's eyes, even Dad's, welled up in tears. It was hard to grapple with the fact that my brother, of all people, had pledged eternal love while also taking on the responsibility of raising Sally's hyperkinetic seven-year-old son, Johnny.

The Tharpe family was educated; Grammie Hall nailed them as "upper-crust types." While waiters passed out drinks, she quietly sat next to George. After a few glasses of wine, Grammie Keaton, quite giddy, roamed around congratulating everyone. The food, prepared by Phillip, a caterer from San Diego, was delicious. The whole Tharpe family, including Sally's sisters, Robin and DeDe, and even her brother, Robert, changed into more casual clothes after the ceremony. It seemed sort of weird to us common folk, but we didn't care. We were having a great time.

Randy couldn't have been in better spirits. I mingled,

checking out the cabin, looking for Sally's touches. The weather was perfect.

The guests were continuing to share laughs while taking in the lovely atmosphere when Grammie Hall suddenly fell on the cobblestone steps leading to the patio.

George bent down and tried to help her up as Dad rushed over. "Mom, don't worry, you're all right. You're all right. Let her go, George. It's okay."

Grammie, flat on her back, kept repeating, "I've broken my hip. Is my arm broken too? I think I've broken my hip. I didn't see the steps. Why did you let me go, George?"

George, breathless and shaking, whispered, "I couldn't hold you, Mary. You're gonna be all right. I'm sorry."

It was heartbreaking to see Grammie crying on the ground in her Ivers royal-blue pantsuit. After making sure she didn't have a broken bone, Dad helped her get into my car. Once the three of us were inside, she turned toward me with that infamous hawklike gaze. "Have your fun while you're young, Diane," she said.

Once we arrived at Grammie's duplex, I went downstairs to get some ice cubes. On the way back, I saw Gram sitting on a chair while George gently tried to unbutton her blouse. She seemed to look at him with affection. I realized it was the only time I had witnessed any kind of intimacy, perhaps even love, between the two.

Before I left, George handed me a couple of bucks to buy some gas. I kissed him, kissed Gram, and walked out of the kitchen, wondering if Randy would be a "till death do us part" kind of guy like George.

Glued into one of Mom's scrapbooks, a creamy-looking photograph documenting Randy's marriage to Sally fills the last page. In the center of the frame, two families are united. Dorrie, Robin, and I stand next to Judge Tharpe and his wife. The seated guests in front include little Johnny, Grandmother Tharpe, Grammie Keaton, and Grammie Hall. Everyone appears lost within a soft-focus blur—everyone with the exception of middle-aged Jack Hall, standing in the shadow of a low-hanging tree with his left arm wrapped around Dorothy's waist. Mom looks at Randy, whose arm, like Dad's, is wrapped around the waist of his new wife. Sally's hand reassuringly clasps his as they smile into the future. In that moment, at least to me, both men unabashedly shared the same feeling of love.

To me this photograph captures the power a woman can have over a man. Even though Mom and Dad's journey became more challenging with time, it was always defined by an undying, if sometimes fractured commitment. Jack and Dorothy were sharing one of life's great moments of hope. Their son had married a substantial young woman who loved him. In a way, they were "living truthfully," as Sandy Meisner would have said, "in a moment of fiction."

Six months after Randy's wedding, it was George's turn to fall. He landed on Grammie's linoleum floor in the room he'd rented for thirty years and began hemorrhaging. As he clutched his stomach in a fetal position, I wonder, did he think of all the pigeons he'd fed out of his hand? Dear George. Life moves on. Love is transient. Men need women, even tough-as-nails women like Mary Hall, or complex romantics like Mom. As for George, he passed on without so much as a wave goodbye to his longtime companion, Mary Hall. The grown-up Hall kids missed out on the opportunity to see George perform one last card trick in Grammie's living room.

Grammie's response to George's all-too-soon, permanent departure from the bedroom off the narrow hallway was summed up in one sentence: "He never gave me a nickel." When asked about her own death, she said, "I'm not afraid of dying. There ain't much to it. You can go crazy thinking about it. I say don't be overactive in thinking because you can overact so much you'll get the mind going haywire." At least, that's what Mom wrote down in one of her journals. Grammie lived to be ninety-four.

Years later, I found a short poem Randy wrote about her. If she'd had the opportunity to read it, would she have understood, as Mom did, that he saw the world through the eyes of a dreamer?

Her long hands stay with me in the dying days of summer.
I see them in the dried out gardens of abandoned homes,
I see them when I close my eyes to forget.
The thin light of their touch slides through me like narrow branches.
What is this gift the dying give?

Life went on. Robin and Dorrie kept me abreast of everything. Dad confessed to them he could only get near one person in his whole life: "Your Mud." Robin mentioned that Sally took Mom aside, wanting to know if she would approve of her and Randy having a baby—she was feeling "motherish." Mom, of course, was overjoyed. She described how Randy'd come home, take his shoes and socks off, pull his shirt out, look at Sally, and say, "Hi, Dumbkus. Got any beer?" When Johnny asked him if he could stay up until ten-thirty to watch TV, Randy responded with "I'm pretty sure you're smart enough to have figured that out by now." Sally joined in, "No use pouting, Johnny, you know when bedtime is." It was almost like he'd become a junior version of Dad.

In 1974, a year after the wedding, I was in New York City, preparing to film *The Godfather: Part II,* when I got a letter from Dorrie describing how Randy's too-good-to-be-true scenario was beginning to crumble.

Dear Diane,

I'm spending a couple of nights in Silverado Canyon. Immaculate Heart College will be starting soon, so I have to enlist mom's help in buying a bed, number one, but also getting books and finding a desk and everything else. I'll have to share an apartment with a roommate. I'm a little freaked out. Speaking of freaked out . . . Randy seems to be very scared these days. He and Sally almost broke up over his irresponsiveness. Sally said he needs her out of one thing only: loneliness. There's nothing romantic on his side. His main worry is that he can't handle working for Dad anymore. He's afraid he might totally lose it. He's scared. It's a bad scene.

Love, Dorrie

Several months later, Robin called to say that Sally had recently had lunch with Mom and told her she intended to leave Randy after Christmas, that he was semi-crazy. She spoke of a so-called waking fantasy he had of killing women. I tried to imagine Mom's response to such an accusation. A fantasy of killing women? She must have tossed the absurd concept aside, because I never heard it brought up again. Sally wouldn't actually leave Randy until a few years later.

In his journals, Randy wrote his own response to the split in an unusually long narrative passage.

I began those couple of years in the canyon driving into Orange County every morning to work for my father as a draftsman. I drove back in the evenings to a rented, single-story log cabin I shared with Sally. In late 1975 she and I were still bell-bottomed and long haired. We thought of our place as back-to-earth hip. We felt certain a new way of life had been paved by the revolution of the sixties. In our cabin, the kitchen and bedroom doors held bright strings of hanging beads. The living room, with its large potted plants, leather and wooden furniture, smelled almost as woody as the outdoors. Zen Buddhism and diet were a high priority. We ate brown rice and raw vegetables. Pot and wine were smoked and sipped in the evenings with the belief that wisdom came from the earth. It sure seemed like wisdom as Sally and I would sit outside on our worn out leather couch, and listen to the river.

I'd park the VW in the open garage built beneath

our living room, run up the brick steps to the picket fence, and hurry across the wet grass to find Sally standing in the doorway under a yellow light. We'd hug and kiss then step inside, closing the door behind us. God, she looked great in a long green dress that followed her curves down to the ankles of her feet. "Randy, do you want a glass of wine before dinner?" she'd say walking to the kitchen, her backside shifting deliciously. "Yeah. And a fat joint. It's been a year now, and those dickheads at the office are getting on my nerves." I'd sit on the couch, exhale loudly, close my eyes and wait for her [to] hand me a cold, tall glass, place the joint in a clean seashell ashtray and set it on the coffee table in the center of our crowded living room. "Can't you talk to your father?" she said, laying one arm around my shoulders. "Are you kidding? He's one of them." After a while she replied, "He seems nice enough to me. I think he can be really funny." I turned my face to her. "You don't see him at work." Sally kissed me on the nose, her olive green eyes, slightly dilated, sparkled like damp glass. "When's dinner ready? I'm starved."

We flew (I do not use that word lightly) into the early summer months of 77. Sally had cut her hair. She was sexier than ever. It had something to do with her neck. I had never noticed how glorious a throat could be. She added chicken to our diet. We took to smoking hashish through a terra cotta, toad-shaped pipe. Our fights began to increase. They were always the same. I was always quick to fall silent. She hated that, screamed at the ceiling, and ran to the stereo for distraction. Moments later music would come thumping loud and clear through the cabin. It drove me nuts. It made her cry. An hour later I'd come back to a quiet house and find her cleaning an already clean kitchen. "You don't fight fair," she'd say. "I'm sorry," I'd answer, feeling unhinged about my liabilities. Then she'd walk up to me and sink her tongue in my mouth as if she were mining for gold. After each rift we'd hold hands watching the canyon surrender its color to shadows. Sally always spoke first, her voice liquid and dreamy. "Let's make love, Randy." I'd smile as she slipped off her jeans and t-shirt with a single handed agility that never failed to amaze me. Then with the picket fence as our only source of privacy, we'd cling to each other, my clothes coming off slowly, her eyes burning with determination.

My situation at work was unbearable. I found myself downing beer while driving home to ease the disastrous state of my nerves. But I couldn't quit. The money was too good. One Friday evening I sat at the kitchen table with a shot glass of brandy as Sally talked non-stop about her new job as a florist. The words kept flowing as she placed the stew before me and settled into a chair at the other end of the table. The second our eyes met I knew I hadn't hidden my disinterest. She frowned and fell silent. The room seemed to darken. For a full ten minutes the sound of chewing and swallowing filled the air. "I'm sorry," I said. "Oh

Christ! Shall I write that down?" she growled. Then, with unexpected calm, she scooted her chair around the table and sat next to me, put a hand on my shoulder and squeezed softly. I wept instantly. It had nothing to do with my miserable job. It was in response to the power and meaning of her gesture. For the past year I had been oblivious to the changes in her behavior. Sally had grown up. I'd remained nothing more than an oversized stupid child. A burden.

We stayed together another nine months. Sally loved her work and soon became manager of the shop. We bought another used VW so she wasn't bound to my schedule. Her manner of dress turned conservative. I must admit she looked nothing less than stunning. As her world was expanding, mine was diminishing. She made new friends, gave small dinner parties in which the conversation was so absorbed with work oriented details I had to make quick exits. I'd walk down to the river, cross the gravel bridge to the main road leading in and out of the canyon. Hurrying up to where the asphalt ended, I'd climb over the fence with a no trespassing sign hanging on its locked gate. My secret place was a large flat stone jetting out over a small waterfall which, in heavy rains pounded over the rock platform with a tumbling white rage. I'd sit knowing I was going to quit my job the minute Sally stopped feeling sorry for me, and eased herself out the door with a clear conscience. Lying back, relief, not sorrow swept over me. I felt light as a down pillow. The air was always eucalyptus sweet, and the stars in heaven shone brighter than before. If there were any heartaches lurking inside me, they had nothing to do with relationships and everything to do with leaving the canyon life behind.

Randy wrote these entries in his journal almost two years following the split. He never mentioned Johnny. It was as if he didn't exist. If he'd been able to communicate to us at the time, maybe we would have been able to help. Maybe his next steps would have been different. But, then again . . . we never bothered to discuss the Sally situation. It was too painful. Perhaps, along with Sally and her son, Johnny, we were all a source of tiresome conflict not worth examining.

After Sally split, Robin called to tell me Randy had withdrawn more than ever. Dad talked about him at breakfast one morning and started crying. She'd never seen him cry before. He didn't know what to do, he said.

When Randy didn't show up at work for a couple of weeks, Dad drove to Silverado to see him. He talked about the situation at the office, reminding Randy that Hall and Foreman was carrying his health insurance; it couldn't easily be reinstated if dropped. He tried to convey his concerns for Randy in a caring way, wanted him to know he understood what Randy was reaching for and would help support him if he knew what Randy wanted to do.

Randy indicated he was searching for a different direction in his life. He wanted to occupy himself with activities that didn't give him such angry feelings. He told Dad he was proud of his writing and pleased to have taken up creating a series of collages.

And that was it. A month went by and Randy didn't come back. Dad was still waiting for his call. Mom didn't hear from him, either. It was as if he had dropped out of sight, like a missing person.

It could be said that Randy's passivity for such a long time, exacerbated by too much fear, had caused permanent anger. Now he'd finally done something about it; he'd made his position clear.

Fifty-six-year-old Dorothy continued having faulty judgments about Randy's future. The progression of her marriage stayed the same, in spite of endless pep talks to herself on paper that effectively took away responsibility for examining her anger. She kept up with her journals, scrapbooks, and photography, but they did not sustain her. I wonder when the concept of wishing took over more practical methods of dealing with envy, low self-esteem, comparison, and the resulting depressions, which were glossed over as Randy's mental status declined. When all hell broke loose over Randy's breaking up with Sally, and quitting his job in the midst of a breakdown, I worried about her. Why did she insist everything was going to get better? Her resolve to "think positive" without exploring the next step was numbing.

I guess her endless repetitive journal entries soothed her. "I'm still sending poems out for Randy, but things are slack. This will change." "My photo work will start up with a bang." "Randy's work will be accepted by many publications." "I'm

on the track with Randy—his poems are getting acclaimed."
"Randy is making headway with his poetry—and even more
will be coming." "I have great green positive go thoughts
for this year of 77. I honestly believe this goes for all of us.
Me, Jack, Diane, Randy, Robin, and Dorrie. This means the
responsibility of success, money, good feelings in ways physi-
cal, mental and spiritual." "Randy got an accept from Rocky
Mountain Review—2 poems 'Salamander' and 'Alchemist.'"
"Good news. Randy's 'Pervert' was accepted by New Orleans
Review."

Meanwhile, back in New York, I'd earned enough money
to move out of my rental and buy an apartment in the San
Remo, overlooking Central Park West. But the truth is, I
didn't feel comfortable in my new shoes. I was lonely. Success
was a confusing dream come true. 1976's *I Will . . . I Will . . .
for Now* had opened to a host of bad reviews, including Roger
Ebert's: "I don't often look at my watch during a movie, but I
found myself consulting it closely during 'I Will . . . I Will . . .
for Now.' Could it be possible that this dreck still had an hour
to go? The film moves at a leaden pace, interrupted only by
its dead halts, and the actors stand around looking appalled at
themselves after being forced to recite dialog like, 'I still love
that hard-nosed little dumpling.' Diane Keaton is so painfully
sincere, we're not even sure some scenes are supposed to be
funny. There will be worse movies this year, but probably none
so stupefying."

My response? I followed suit with Randy, making collages
and writing until the next movie, whatever it might be. In 1977,
my own journal was filled with short, depressing entries such

as: "Art Linkletter's daughter Diane jumped out a window to experience death's calling." "I carry a wallet full of evidence; a mouth brimming with lies. My face is open to deceit, deception and plain old . . . apathy." "Woody has taken to buying cigarettes. He carries a pack in his pocket. He takes one out, flips it into his mouth with a false sense of bravado, and smokes without inhaling. He says it gives his hands something to do."

With Mom's approval, Dad came up with what he thought might be a solution for Randy's broken marriage. He went out and bought a two-story town house on Tangerine Street in Irvine, in a gated community for swinging singles. When he handed Randy the key, including a brochure illustrating swinging single life at its best, Dad must have thought his gift would be the path to a new beginning for his son. In the colorful pamphlet, photographs illustrated young adults gathered by a pool, forming new relationships as they barbecued hamburgers in front of the community center. I can only imagine how insane it must have been for Randy. The promise of "Single Living at Its Best" in Irvine, a then bright new city in Orange County, gave Dad a sense of hope. Unfortunately, he hadn't noticed the presence of El Toro Marine Base's West Coast fighter squadrons flying over the rooftops of Tangerine Street. For Randy, it was as if he'd been thrust into his toddler past, filled with Lockheed T-33's and F-104's marking the skies of Bushnell Way Road. The sobbing little towheaded boy screaming for Mom had come back to haunt him.

Unaware that Tangerine Street was a destination that fit all of Randy's prerequisites for failure, Jack Hall must have thought that securing Randy's finances in a safe community would protect him from harm, while also giving him a chance to recover—a chance to come back to Hall and Foreman a new man, engaged in extracurricular activity with other young adults. But it was there, in that stucco two-story town house, that Randy permanently rid himself of a so-called life of normalcy, where he made his one and only permanent vow: to engage his life in the company of beer and vodka. He was twenty-seven years old.

CHAPTER 6

PRINTERS PULL OFF A GOOD ONE

Gary Young went to high school with Randy. Later, he moved to Santa Cruz, where he became a professor at the University of California while also spearheading the Greenhouse Review Press. In 1977, he printed a little book of Randy's poems called *The Dreams of Mercurius.* It even got reviewed by Stephen Kessler, who is the editor and publisher of *The Redwood Review:*

> *The Dreams of Mercurius,* a book of a dozen tiny poems by southern California poet John Hall, is the latest and most interesting publication yet to emerge from the Greenhouse Review Press, worthy of attention not only for its content and its quality as a finely crafted object of the printer's art but for its manifestation of a poetic alternative to the popular trend of more personal writing. In the *Dreams of Mercurius* there are subtle things going on, more fragile investigations of an

alchemical nature, a delicate raid on the realm of trans-formation. The book's first poem is called "Smoke."

> *Incense fills the room*
> *with peach blossoms.*
> *Beneath a thousand petals*
> *the moon slides down the window.*
> *The opium is wet leaves and earth.*
> *You fill your lungs*
> *and mountains are crowned with glass.*

The oriental depth and simplicity of this poem, the richly suggestive directness of its statement, drifts through the reader's mind precisely like the smoke of its title. Peach blossoms, petals, moon, window, leaves and earth are fused in this final image, all a result of the smoke of its title and work like a drug to conjure a gently hallucinatory image: mountains "crowned with glass." Such simple elements combining to dis-close the curious interpenetration of interior and exte-rior worlds—the human body, the room, the sky, the moonlit mountains—are a marvelous example of a poem's power to alter consciousness, to show us the secret relations of things, to give us a wholeness of perception not always available to our everyday aware-ness. *The Dreams of Mercurius* is a fine beginning.

In her journal, Mom wrote, "Randy's Chap Book, Dreams of Mercurius, was handed to me today—Gary Young published 300 copy's. This is a goal I've directed long moments of thought toward him for years, and this is only the beginning."

Stephen Kessler's review had a great effect on both Mom and Randy. I don't remember paying too much attention. I'd been overwhelmed with work and had just been in *Looking for Mr. Goodbar.* I remember being happy for Randy, but wondering why one of the more oblique poems was his choice for the title. Mercurius, a god of abundance and success, also served as a guide to newly deceased souls entering the afterlife. Success and abundance, like the kind Dad worked so hard for? Guiding the dead to an afterlife? I didn't get it. Anyway, I didn't have time to elaborate. The opportunity the director Richard Brooks had given me to play Theresa Dunn, a masochistic young woman unconsciously seeking out death while looking for love in all the wrong places, consumed me. Meanwhile, Mom couldn't resist sending me a brand-new poem, one that Randy had just finished:

> *In the field beneath the Milky Way,*
> *beneath the darkness, cool & perfect,*
> *lying like a great whale*
> *beached in a dream,*
> *I listen to the owl*
> *lift out of the sycamores*
> *and cry like a soft white bell—*

Dear Randy,
This is a completely beautiful interpretation of an observation. I'm overwhelmed at the twist of fate

which made me one-half of a genetic act bringing you
into life. I'm proud to be your parent because of what
it means in terms of who you are. I feel this rumbling
inside me every time I read your work. I don't like
to call them "poems" because that word has a tone
of frothy, mind wanderings, and I don't in any way
equate that to what you write. I'm sorry I have such a
difficult time expressing myself regarding your work,
which is of great importance. I dread the day when
I won't be a part of your poetic process, but I realize
it will come, and I promise to deal with that when it
happens. I admire the way you ignore us dullards who
get a gleeful expression as we tell you of misspelled
words, etc. . . . like that's of such importance. What
silly needs we have. Don't ever lower yourself to our
level—technical correctness is mechanical, but your
words are the precision tools of a genius.

Love, Mom

Excited by Randy's success, Mom enlisted me to send a batch
of his new poems to my friend Larry McMurtry, for his
take.

Dear Diane,
I've been reading your brother's poems. There's quite
a bit of technical variety in them, lots of wonderful
rhetoric. They would make an interesting book, and
yet there's a direction to most of the poems that's

limiting them. I can't tell whether it's accidental,
temperamental or what. Most of them have an
iconic strategy: he sets up a figure (potter, gardener,
fisherman, saint) and, in establishing the icon, often
sort of blocks the poem from getting really particular.
He seems to go naturally to the "you" poem, the
second person voice, but in about half a dozen poems,
he allows the "I" to come in. These poems are much
more impressive and dramatic, I think, though I'm
not simply equating the "I" with Randy. In reading a
whole group of them, one gets a sense of a guy sort of
directing the reader away from himself. He's hesitant
to use his own personality. Yet, when he does, or
seems to, it works very strongly. I'm still digesting.
He wrote a couple of quite good poems. Randy sure
moves on his own track, and no other.

 Love, Larry

Randy was spared Larry's response, but not Mom's, which
was, as expected, glowing:

Dear Randy,
Your poem silverado canyon has moved me to the
point of wanting to write you a long, personal epistle
about my thoughts concerning you and your writing,
but most especially the effect your words have on me.
As I read your delicately worded poem I got a vivid
picture of you and the complexities of your thinking.

I can only imagine what it must be like to have a
vision of the world that expresses itself in thoughts
like:

ONCE UPON A TIME

Father is doing a handstand on the beach.
His thin, muscular legs dangle backwards over his head.
Once, a long time ago I studied the photograph.
His face was not where it should be.
Even after turning the picture upside down something was wrong;
How could he hold the world in the palms of his hands?
It frightened me then. It frightens me now.
Father upset nature. At least in my mind he did.

After staying away for as long as he could, Randy returned
to Hall and Foreman. Just like old times, Dad tried to hide
the disappointment he felt about Randy from Hugh and the
employees, but he incessantly griped about him to Mom. Mom
had moved to a higher plane in her defense of Randy. As she'd
said in her letter to him, she truly believed he was a genius.
That word, "genius," for her was an irrefutable shield against
the ordinary expectations of people like Dad. Given her own
dreams, it must have been a place she, too, would have liked to
take refuge.

Decades later, on a phone call with Randy, I tried to get
him to talk about Dad. He didn't bite, but days later wrote me:

I don't have a pleasant memory of Dad. I was afraid of him the whole time. Remember when he spanked us, and we had to pull down our pants before he whacked our bottoms? I'll never forget running around clutching my butt screaming. He was sadistic. You have to admit he had a sadistic nature. And I wonder where I got mine!!!! Even way back, even then I knew he didn't get me. He would pounce on me for the weirdest reasons. Like with math. He'd ask me what one times one was. I'd say, "Two." "Pull your head out of the sand." That's what he'd say. He'd say, "Pull your head out of the sand. It's one." "How come it's one and not two?" I asked. He actually slapped me on that one. What did I do wrong? Why was he so pissed? I didn't get it, so I didn't say it right, so what? He made me feel like I didn't know anything. I'll tell you this. There was no way I was going to become his civil engineer son, that's for damn sure. And those weird Toastmaster's events where we were supposed to give speeches on subjects relating to success. Well, guess what, Dad wasn't as brave as he made himself out to be. He too was nervous before going on. He would shake, just like me. He would shake like a leaf. Sure, he fought through all that fear, but it made for a tight, unlovable person. Money was everything to him. He kept making money and more money; that's what he did. There was no telling what he was going to do. He proved it later on when he threatened to leave me down at the tip of Baja on a motorcycle trip he thought would bring us closer together. I was only 19. God, I hated that. Sometimes, I think Mom hated him too, especially when he would say things that made her fume, she'd get so mad she'd just shut up. Remember? I mean, she wouldn't speak for a whole evening. One time he tore the door off the bathroom just to get at her. Now that's anger. Dad scared me. If I did something wrong, if I was clumsy, if I was not thinking ahead, if I did not have a game plan, or an approach to say, peeling an orange, there would be trouble. If my fumbling hands made me puncture the pith of the skin so the juice dripped out he would lose it. He didn't have patience with my awkwardness. He wanted precision in the world, and, from me, less meaningless talk.

I remember thinking about the significant difference between Randy's and my relationships to our father. Not only was I lucky enough to be a girl, free from the crushing expectations Dad had for a son; I also had a dream. My dream had nothing to do with Dad's world of precision and expertise. I wanted to be a movie star. I wanted people—lots of people I didn't know—to love me.

On March 27, 1977, *Annie Hall* was screened at Filmex, the Los Angeles International Film Exhibition. Mom wrote in her journal:

The theater was flooded with lights and fireworks overhead. It was a big deal for the closing night. Inside the theater was packed. We sat on steps at the back of the room. *Annie Hall*. An evaluation is always hard for me on the first viewing. I only saw Diane, her mannerisms, speech pattern, expressions, dress, hair, etc. the total her. The plot, the story, the photography, and sets took second place. I'll have to wait for the second or third screening to see what I really think. When she sang "It Had to Be You" in a room full of talk and confusion I fought back tears. The song, "Seems Like Old Times," was a hard one to take—so tender, I was exploding inside while trying to hold it all back. She looked beautiful all the way through. Gordon Willis did a very great job on the photography. Diane chose her own clothes. The gray T shirt and baggy pants were "down home" for sure. In reality *Annie Hall* is a love story, covering six years in the life of Woody Allen and Diane Hall Keaton. The screenplay ended up with many things differing from the truth, even though it seemed all too real. Annie's camera in hand, her gum chewing, her lack of confidence—pure Diane. Woody Allen's all too human love story, while tender, funny, and sad ended in separation, just like it did in real life.

The Hall family was depicted as funny, especially Duane, a thinly disguised substitute for Randy. Duane [played by Christopher Walken] was a sensitive person with a unique personality Woody's character couldn't cope with. Colleen Dewhurst playing me was not a high spot. She didn't come off well. Grammie Hall was a sight gag. Jack's part was not impressive, or appealing.

The audience loved it all. This will certainly be a very popular movie.

After Woody and I went our separate ways, Warren Beatty came into my life. It was a new world order. People, politics, endless conversations late into the night with the likes of Gary Hart, Elaine May, Robert Towne, and Jack Nicholson, to name a few. Warren, with the help of others, was almost finished with his script about John Reed, the American journalist, poet, and socialist activist, best remembered for *Ten Days That Shook the World,* his firsthand account of the Bolshevik Revolution. I was going to play Louise Bryant, an ambitious, free-loving left-wing journalist. A few days before flying off to England to begin filming *Reds,* we shared a meal with Mom and Dad. Later, Warren described Dad as part loner, part charmer. He thought he had a "boyish" way about him. Warren took note of our similarities. Apparently, I also had Jack's glad-handing, greeter-type appeal that couldn't sustain endless conversations.

At the Easter Sunday dinner in *Annie Hall,* Mr. Hall, a stiff Republican, talks about going out to the boat basin with his son, Duane, where they loved to caulk holes. Our fictional family were middle-class white Americans who didn't get sick. I doubt Dad appreciated the depiction, but at least he had the grace never to mention it. Besides, he had enough on his plate with Hall and Foreman.

It's hard to imagine what working for Dad must have been like for Randy, especially after his split with Sally. Being the boss's son was a humiliation that enhanced Randy's determination to be left alone at any expense. As a partial surveyor, updating boundary lines and preparing sites for construction, Randy provided the necessary data relevant to the shape and contour of the earth's surface, but he was always making mistakes. One day, Dad called Randy into his office and insisted he refer to him as Mr. Hall in front of the employees. This was the straw that broke the camel's back, but, as usual, Randy didn't say a word. He just disappeared again, this time into the town house on Tangerine.

Mom was riddled with concern when she wrote: "Randy's into his 4th week of silence. He's unplugged his phone. On Easter Sunday, I called to see if he was going to Grammie Hall's with us. He said if he wasn't here by 11 AM, to go without him. I haven't heard from him since. Once there, Grammie Hall asked Dorrie if Randy was hitting the bottle because all too soon he was going to run out of money."

Mom left messages on his answering machine, suggesting solutions and offering possibilities. Randy remained unresponsive. Instead, he drank bottles of Scotch and wrote about his conflicting feelings with regard to his great champion and defender:

My mother is a ghost to me, a pale Methodist phantom conjured up from the flat lands of Kansas. We floated in each other's lives like broken compasses. I have gone nowhere. No, that is not true; I have gone to the land of muted rage, spectral skirts and disembodied voices. I would have preferred a bitch for a mother, someone solid and distasteful—at least there would be a center, a place I could leave. Mother is a puff of smoke shape-shifting in my blood.

There is always something wrong. Our conversations never jibe. I don't know what she really means. Strangely enough we're very close; two sailors at sea clinging to the wreckage of our ship but silent in our camaraderie, silent in the sense that she speaks Chinese and I speak Turkish. Yesterday she called me on the phone. "Randy, it's your mom. Hi. Are you writing? Why don't you send me some?" (Because, mother, you never understand what I've written and it is embarrassing to hear you say that you do.) "Well, I just called to see how you were doing. You're okay aren't you?" "Yes, mother." And that was it. She evaporated. I think of her, after such conversations, as a dream that beats the body to exhaustion, a dream repeated throughout a lifetime.

Randy wasn't the only one hitting the bottle. Late one night, after enjoying a few too many vodka-and-sodas, while speeding through Balboa Bay in their new catamaran, Mom and Dad were surprised when the Harbor Patrol sounded a warning to turn off the engine. An argument ensued. Dad took things into his own hands, gunned the engine, and split. When the authorities caught up, he turned off the power, jumped into the water, and swam home, leaving Mom behind on the boat. Once Dad arrived home, the police showed up with handcuffs. The president of Hall and Foreman was sent to jail for the rest of the night.

In the fall of 1980, while I was in London filming Warren Beatty's *Reds,* Robin, a newly certified registered nurse visiting Mom and Dad, called me long distance. In a panic, she said she'd awoken to find Dad sleeping downstairs on the floor. Mom had red marks on her face. The door to their bedroom was knocked off its hinges. Neither Mom nor Dad explained what had happened, and she was too frightened to ask. As if that wasn't enough, later the same day, she took Mom to see Randy at the Tangerine Street condo. They knocked on the door; no response. Mom had the key, so they let themselves in. The kitchen counters were filthy. The grime in the sink was a quarter-inch thick. The walls had holes in them. There were empty liquor bottles everywhere. Light fixtures had been torn off the wall—and the smell—the smell was unbearable. It was a dire situation.

Mom and Dad were clearly in trouble, but in her journal she kept her focus on her son:

Randy hasn't worked since February. I'm sick with frustration. He's dropped out of touch with everyone except Dr. Markson, a psychiatrist Jack finally let me hire to help. He's taken the phone cord out of the wall, and totally withdrawn. I've been to see him twice. Both times he assured me he was all right, saying he wasn't depressed, just working some things out. He's through with Hall and Foreman—what he will do next is a mystery. How will he support himself? I could scream from pain. I feel as if I failed somewhere, or all along. When Jack asked $300.00 rent of him

Randy sent it, which must leave him near the bottom.
My head & heart are taxed to the limit. The girls and I
talk about the problem, but not Jack. He won't go into
it at all. A change has to take place soon.

I'd been busy making films, more than ten of them in ten
years. One of those years was spent living in London, shooting *Reds*. While I acted my way through movie after movie,
my brother's decade was spent drinking inside his trashed-out
swinging-singles condo, with low-flying fighter jets terroriz-
ing him day in and day out. Years later, he told me how desper-
ate he'd been: while I was playing the firebrand Louise Bryant,
he'd attempted to gas himself in the garage. At the time, despite
worried reports from Robin and Dorrie, I'd chosen to justify
my absence by being ensconced in a life that enlarged my hori-
zons. I told myself I didn't have time to linger on my family's
problems, and certainly not Randy's.

Dad made a move to stop all assistance. But Mom couldn't
live with the idea of Randy facing the world without help.
Randy didn't have a job. Could he even handle one? His appearance was getting worse. He'd quickly gained a lot of weight. He
didn't give "a rat's fuck," as Dad put it, about the way he looked,
or anything else. Dad argued that Randy's freefall was not
something they should fund. Mom eventually won out: Randy
never had to work again. Jack Hall accepted his fate by issuing
Randy a monthly stipend for the rest of my father's life. Randy
couldn't have cared less about being the so-called bum Dad tor-
tured himself over. He didn't have the foresight to comprehend
he'd gone too far into the woods to find a path back. Instead,

Randy took failure and wore it the way Hester Prynne wore her scarlet letter. At thirty-five, he proudly took on the role of a destitute man who appeared to have been raised by wolves.

Strangely enough, after the release of *Reds,* he wrote me a letter. It was first time he'd ever written me anything that commented on my acting.

Diane,
I think you outdid yourself. You've done great acting in other films, but there are times in "Reds" when I wanted to stop the projector so the moment wouldn't move so fast. Where did you learn to use your face so well? I think you ran across every emotion in the book, then threw the book away and made up some of your own. It comes off the screen like some magical honey. Anyhow, you did yourself good and you can take pride, not only in the film, but of your contribution. (This is not idle chatter. I really believe it.)
Randy

Writing continued to be the medium Randy expressed himself in. He wrote and wrote and wrote. Letters, poems, fantasy-driven stories. Several stick out from that time:

Billy Seven Fingers had a wicked father whose name was Fat Boy Todder. On Tuesday he punished his son with silver tools while Billy screamed and fingers flew. When Billy grew up he killed Fat Todder with electric wires and bathtub water. Billy buried Fat Boy near an orange tree where every morning he goes to pee.

Here's Uncle George under an apricot tree, feeding a blue jay with an open hand. The bird is perched on his fingertips, its head cocked to one side. You can see George's teeth protruding from a wide grin. George is sixty years old and knows he is dying. He spent his last six months coaxing hope out of the sky and feeding it.

Truth is I was one scared shitless kid who cried on the first day of school and ran out of the classroom three times before Mother was allowed to take me home. Truth is my father stuck a broom handle up my ass simply by calling my name. Truth is I died at the age of ten but just kept walking around wondering who would slap me next. Truth is my mother lay naked in the bathtub while I asked her questions about my home work as I peeked at her breasts. Truth is I was a chip-off-the-old-block that quickly turned to sand under my father's heels as he stomped his way to a for-tune. Truth is I grew up confused by passion and con-fused by desire so much so I hated my flesh and feared my thoughts. Perhaps part of my brain was missing at birth. Truth is the doctors replaced it with fish gut and extension cords. Truth is the sadness inside my head was shrapnel from a distant parental war or maybe lack of supervision. The truth? My family was, and is, a crowd of strangers.

CHAPTER 7

BIRDMAN

By the mid-1980s, when Randy I were both in our thirties, we'd stopped sharing experiences. My success was an uncomfortable reality I didn't know how to navigate. Instead of retreating back to the familiar terrain of my family, once again I pulled away. I sensed that my absence, coupled with such good fortune, may have caused regret for Mom, maybe even for Dad. Still, I once more convinced myself I didn't have time to engage with their ongoing plight to save Randy.

In 1986, while shooting the film *Crimes of the Heart* in North Carolina, I had a day off and decided to visit the Tregembo Animal Park in Wilmington. I remember coming across a cassowary stuck in a small cage. His massive body seemed too big for such short legs. Bright-blue feathers peppered with chunks of orange stuck out from his dark-gray plumage. Unkempt and uncomfortable, he looked like he was about to topple over. As I read the brief description outside his tiny enclosure, I learned that in the humid rain forest the strange bird was quite adept at disappearing. I had to smile. The cassowary, I thought, isn't so different from Randy—or me, for that matter.

Randy was still living on Tangerine Street, still unemployed, and still hoping for more publications. The screaming jets flying above continued to drive him crazy. From Randy's point of view, Dad had bought the Tangerine Street town house to make sure he would suffer. Mom privately met with his psychiatrist, Dr. Markson. After a while, she felt comfortable enough to open up her thoughts and feelings. She told him that Jack was convinced Randy was the source of all their misery. She claimed that if he had any feelings for his son he would be more empathetic. Nothing had changed. It was as if they were stuck in an endless Sandy Meisner Repetition Game.

In her journal from June 1989, Mom described an unexpected call from Randy. Dad answered, began arguing with him, and slammed the phone down. Mom drove to Randy's town house in an effort to patch things up. Randy, well into his drinks, confessed that he was beginning every day with a six-pack of beer, followed by tequila at night. Yes, he knew it was bad, but he couldn't quit. Mom called Dr. Markson, who told her point-blank that Randy needed to be hospitalized and also told her where to take him.

As soon as Dad got wind of the costs at the Capistrano by the Sea Hospital rehab, there was the expected blowup. "That's 10 thousand dollars and 80 cents a month thrown down a rat hole," Mom quoted him. "He's shined me on for years and I've had it. I'm through. He can go to work just like everyone else has to."

Mom reiterated how much Randy needed help. Dad started yelling. She ran outside, gave it some thought, came back, and pleaded with him to stick by Randy through thick and thin. Dad, still furious, ended the conversation with "He trashed a house we own. He's never said thanks for anything I did for him. I'm not going to support him anymore. Got it!?!"

Later, alone at her desk upstairs, she picked up her pen and wrote in her journal what she'd basically written thousands of times before: Randy was going to get better. He was writing. He would drink less. He would thrive in the healing atmosphere of Capistrano by the Sea. He would dutifully take Buspar, a pill Dr. Markson ordered to treat symptoms of anxiety, and fear.

Randy was admitted two weeks later. At the first group session, the group leader asked how Randy was doing. "Fine," he said. Asked if he would care to expand on that, Randy responded with "Finer." The next day, the group leader told Randy he had to say more than one word. Randy got up and walked out.

It was hard for me to identify with Randy's pain. I couldn't put myself in his shoes. It was easy for me to let him remain in the background of my life. As life went on, Randy occasionally sent me some of the pieces he'd written. One, titled "Seahorse," brought tears to my eyes.

Delicate little creature with the plunger mouth, and beer belly. What is it you ask of me? Yes, I found you in an orange grove frozen in the dirt. Your prickly leather skin caught my eye as I stooped to pick up a fallen orange. How remarkable you were, so far from your tropical home, so strange among the ants and green leaves that surrounded you. I put you in my pocket. Today, nearly three years later, I look at your boney frame, your tiny eyeless sockets and wonder at my love of "death-preserved." Is it my own mortality? One day I too will be frozen in dirt, my bones the only definition of my life. Is that the answer to the question your body forms? On a shelf full of bric-a-brac, you are the only object that once existed, your little shape among stone and glass is a terrifying truth, even a reminder that we come to our God in fear, our bones dripping with answers which our bodies are not ready to accept.

I hadn't thought of Randy's seahorse piece until recently, when I opened the kitchen door and found a fluttering hummingbird on the ground outside. I ran inside to see what I could do for the little thing. Was it hungry? Frantically, I searched the Web to read up on what to feed a hummingbird: place a few drops of nectar on the end of its beak. I didn't have nectar. I decided to boil sugar, put it in an eyedropper, and try to get it down the little guy's throat. After several attempts, I could see it was on its way out of this "old world," as Grammie Hall would have said. And, sure enough, after a few moments it stopped fluttering its wings, and died. I went upstairs, took the small box Mom had made in her silversmithing class at Santa

Ana Junior College, and gently placed its body inside. I put it on the bookshelf in my bedroom. Every morning, as I make my bed, I look at Mom's box, honor the little hummingbird, and thank Randy, whose words have come to be my guide into the exploration of mysteries I've avoided all my life.

OOLOGY (the study of birds' eggs)

A delicate ... is perfected for reasons obvious to anyone with eggs ...ina. The fingers must be narrow, soft and able to fi...through small openning in all but the younger trees, because when said and done, a closed fist in the lab isn't worth an egg in the pan. With steady nerve and careful transport, we label the various markings of such fa... as dodo, dove, duck and ...pper or heron, hobby and honker Then the ...ird part as ...ch is individually wrapped in a ...t b...ke and sent to x-ray for proof of ...ge and estima... release. If there is the sligh... ...t egg is sens...back to its mother and she decides in what fashion it must be raised. This bring out the women in all of us and the sudden urge to nurse anything made of porcelain becomes ...ainful and down right obscene. Work is brought to a halt ...from the doors of ...r building and slide home under ...the secretary of interior who abhors the thought of natural selection, ye... allows us the privilege of wives in whose bodies we c...me ...gether again.

A LAST KISS

On Tuesday, April 3, 1990, Mom wrote:

Robin and I loaded up the car for a few weeks in Arizona. Jack was to follow later in his truck. When we arrived at 10:30 PM we were so tired we couldn't think straight. I called Jack. He was supposed to be on the road. He answered sleepily. "Are you alright?" He said something about not getting ready as fast as he thought he could, he'd decided he would start out the next day. We said goodnight. I went to bed. The next morning I called to see if he was about to begin the eleven hour drive. He said he'd be on the way soon. When I called him late that night he was speaking in vague statements. Robin and I called Dr. Copelan. Upon hearing the symptoms, he told us we needed to get Jack to St. Joseph Hospital for an MRI brain scan as a precaution. I knew Jack would not like the idea of Robin and me flying home for his brain scan. But we did. As soon as we saw Dr. Copelan's face, we knew the news was bad. He told us of two cancer masses located in the frontal lobe of Jack's brain. He showed us the pictures. In no uncertain terms, we needed to drive to UCLA, where a certain Dr. Black would be waiting for us.

In those brief five months of illness, Dad was looked after by an onslaught of caregivers who came and went. Mom had no false hopes of a recovery. The days were filled with duties that drove her half mad. She resented all the people in her home, night and day. She began to rewrite her marriage. Suddenly Dad had been her leader, her friend, her counselor, her courageous husband. She bemoaned the loss of the hands she loved so much. They were not there to hold her. She felt she'd become half a person, wondering how to live out the rest of her life.

Dad didn't want to die; he didn't want to leave a good day behind. He'd spent his entire adult life worrying about his little bunch of dreamers and how they would get by. Not one of us had or has a practical bone in his or her body. Five knuckle-heads. Five useless people at sea in the real world. As head of the family, he had no room for dreams. He had to make sure we were taken care of.

Randy joined our family around the dining-room table on Cove Street in Corona del Mar, in our parents' last house, over-looking Dad's beloved ocean view. We listened to our father try to hold his thoughts together as he described the details of his last will and testament. We all looked on with solemn concern. Dad's greatest legacy, his biggest success, the acquisition of money, would be distributed evenly, but only after Dorothy passed. While he struggled with his words as he tried to describe the allocations, Randy suddenly got up, left the table, and bounded out without so much as a goodbye. He never came back.

Not long after, I was sitting next to my bedridden dad, looking at the waves through his picture window, when he said: "Dianie, did you hear about my biopsy? I was sitting in the audience of this theaterlike room when the doctor asked if there were any people with glyoma, my kind of tumor. So I raised my hand. I told them about the two and a half dollars growing on either side of my brain. This doctor, the chief surgeon, had me come to the stage. I sat in the center and they put a cage over my head, a small cage that fit tight. They hammered something into my skull. They didn't give me anything for the pain. I don't think they did. It hurt some, but mainly the sound of them hammering into my skull bothered me the most. Then they took a needle with an even longer needle inside the needle and injected it into the tumor, so they could take out the fluid and study." Suddenly he stopped talking. He'd noticed something, and turned his head so that he was facing the television set. His favorite show was on, *Major Dad*.

A month later, on September 1, 1990, he died. He was sixty-nine years old.

Randy avoided Dad's memorial. He never called Mom to see how she was doing. He remained silent.

Twenty-eight years later, as I rummaged through my journals trying to piece together Randy's response to our father's
passing, I came across a letter I never sent.

Dear Randy,
You missed Dad's memorial. Robin said he went
like a broken bird. It made me think of all those
sparrows and blue jays mom tried to save over the
years; all those little winged friends who'd flown into
our sliding glass doors, or fell out of the sky for one
unknown reason or another.
   When I'd looked at Dad in his hospital bed just
five months ago he seemed fine except for the bandage
covering a shaved section at the top of his head, and
the long plastic leash filling his body with clear fluid.
It reminded me of those bird feeders you buy at The
Builders Emporium. Dad, like the birds we tried
to save, had a bad fall. Mom said he died facing the
window that framed the ocean slit in half by the blue
of the sky.
   It's hard to imagine what our dying bird saw.
Hands adjusting his head on the pillow? The shadow
of Dorothy's face gliding in for a last kiss? Did death
at the very least grant him a final glimpse of the world
through a hazy blue tint? Do you think he had hopes?
Or was hope a thing with feathers?
   As you know only too well, Dad didn't struggle
to connect through feelings. His words, the things he
said, the lessons he wanted us to learn, constitute a

rigid, blank slate; it's almost as if the spoken word had no place in his relationships. Words were not to be trusted. Perhaps all those multiple meanings led Dad to his almost religious belief in sound bites. Am I on to something here, Randy?

You are one of four people who can help me remember Dad in sentences and paragraphs. You're the only one who's written down your woes on long nights of unhappy days. Remember when we were the only two Hall kids, in diapers? We had a couple of years there when it was just you and me, our bunk bed, and Mom and Dad. Remember how he used to curl up on the beach when he was just a kid himself, when he was still part of an ordinary family making his way to success before all the complications that ensued. Do you remember seeing him so obviously in love with his "Mud"? Maybe the responsibility of accomplishment was too much. All those Toastmasters torture sessions, all those right things to do for the family in order to get ahead. Ahead to what? I know it's been rough for you, Randy. If you'll let me, I'll help you try and remember his eyes spinning visual rhapsodies as he stared, drink in hand, at the waves coming and going for hours at a time. Remember?

When I die, as you know the oldest goes first, I promise to give you a pair of his fins, and the snorkel from the old Bob Blandon skin diving days. I also promise you the striped tie I stole from his closet and the button-down cashmere sweater. Oh, and even all the nickels and dimes he collected in all those jars over the course of a lifetime.

I also intend to include two jars of sand, one from Huntington Beach, the other from Dad's final resting place in Tubac, Arizona. These mementos are for you to remember, not just the difficult times, but the times his face lit up with joy on those rare occasions he let himself appreciate you for who you are. I know I'm reaching here.

What are we, but aspects, infinitesimal aspects, both good and bad, of who our father was. You have to forgive him while you can. Someday we'll be joining him, just a couple more broken birds on our way to where.

Love, Diane

Over the course of several decades, Randy kept hidden a host of impressions based on his perceptions of the father/son relationship. The truth of Randy's unspoken rage in "Letter to Pop from a Suicidal Son" is hard to read, hard to understand, and hard to forgive.

> *Now that you're about to eat the big one,*
> *now that you are curled like a fetus, helpless*
> *in your tent of bone and flesh . . . let me tell*
> *you how I love you; I love your worthlessness,*
> *your money crumbling in its hiding places,*

your body full of drugs that keep you out of my
life. I love your clothes with the stink of your
death. I love the stink of your death, how it sweetens
my life, how it makes you small enough to crush
under foot. Father you are a balloon about to
pop. I love you enough to hold the pin, waiting
to poke you when you open your mouth. Open your
mouth Pop and I'll kill you.

I'm so tired of you, I'm so tired of me. We are
fossil fuel for our own driven madness that feeds on itself.
We have come to an intersection
in which there is nowhere to go; you are turning
toward death. I'm turning toward reluctance.
We are bound to each other but lost to any
reconciliation. Pop, we are fucking Siamese twins,
and I mean that literally, I mean cock-tied. I mean
useless dead things; prehistoric reptilian
flesh turning to oil with unmixable water. I fuck you.
You fuck me, and we are never satisfied. I didn't
start this and when you die, you will not end it,
and for that there is a certain finger I give you long and hard.

I'm spam in a can, dad; food for the populace.
You were the chief slice and dicer.
You took my potential and burnt it,
You carved it into dollar bills and fed it to human
Dogs fresh from the fluff factory. Your death is not only staring
me in the face,

it is eating me inside out.
Sonny Spam is my name, suicide's my game.
And I do so much want to thank you.

Later, among Randy's papers, I found a less tormented perception of their relationship. With time, Randy had had second, even third thoughts. A lifetime of unexplored feelings and memories on the subject of Jack Hall began to creep in.

I will not forget September 1, 1990. A broken bird left the earth. The living could not follow, could not see the wings expand, nor hear the sweet song echo in the heavens. Until now I have never thought of my father as a bird, but something about death makes us small and fragile. "Our father who art in heaven," you trundle us with the wind of your feathers, you make us cry with fear and love. Destination, oh destination, what manner of nest awaits our troubled bodies? If we too are birds what happened to our song in this hour of absence?

And there was this.

Mother gave me his shoes for my birthday saying she had no use for them. They are white Reeboks with long laces and thick off-white soles. They fit me perfectly. When putting them on, I think of my father's feet; Yellow cracked toenails, callused heels. It feels strange to walk in his shoes. Each step echos like a bone striking the taut skin of a drum; each stumble is a forewarning. Yet I continue to wear them, believing a gift is some kind of—any kind of love. Perhaps one day I will nurse the love we never bonded with the love that was always there.

As for Hall and Foreman, Dad's legacy, it continues on as a division of David Evans & Associates. At his memorial service, Hugh Foreman described Dad as having "a great impact on the development of Southern California, especially to the development of Orange County. We shared thirty-five years together as very close friends and associates. It's a sad moment. Losing Jack was like having a right arm cut off." Hugh Foreman said, "You couldn't ask for a more honest partner and associate." Hugh had it right.

CHAPTER 9

THREE SISTERS

After our father's passing, Dorrie became an antiques dealer specializing in Monterey furniture. Robin married, moved to Atlanta, and adopted a baby girl, Riley. Five years later, she adopted a baby boy. She named him Jack. Following Robin's example, I adopted my daughter, Dexter, in 1995, and then my baby boy, Duke, in 2001. One day, over lunch, my friend Nancy Meyers told me she was going to make a movie, and I was going to star in it opposite Jack Nicholson. I told her point-blank she'd lost her mind. Jack Nicholson in a chick flick? No way. Nancy was right, though, and with that lunch my professional life took a turn for the much better, reversing the sharp turn it had recently taken for the worse. In 2001, I starred in a couple of TV movies. In the aptly named *On Thin Ice,* I played Patsy, who turns to dealing drugs and becomes addicted to crystal meth. If that wasn't enough, in *Crossed Over,* the teenage son of my character, Beverly Lowry, is killed by a drunk driver. As she sinks into a deep depression, she forms an unusual friendship with Karla Fay Tucker, the first and only woman executed on death row. Both films proved to be notable failures.

Mom worked at Hunter's Books while volunteering at various charity-owned thrift shops. With her beloved cat, Cyrus, in the backseat of her car, she enjoyed driving to her getaway home in Arizona. She had slowed down quite a bit, but she was still writing in her journals. And she missed Dad. In 1997, she wrote him a letter on Valentine's Day:

Dear Jack,
I regret the things I've learned too late, but I can't
live with regrets. You wouldn't want me to. I look at
couples bickering about some small matter and I want
to say, "Don't take your living time fighting & fussing
over nothing—be happy you have one-another."
I still feel your presence with me, and when that
feeling comes I look up to the sky (as if that's where
you are) and think if I feel you so intensely you must
have a sense of me also. If that's true you know that
I am feeling old. I hate to confront the fact that I'm
slipping in my mental capacities too. It bothers me.
My eyes are weakening even with my recent surgery.
I haven't gone to the dentist for two years and I know
what you would say about that. I am so grateful to
you for the life you gave us, all the comforts and
material things. I am more grateful than I can say.
I'm trying to keep it all going the way you wanted.
You know, of course, that 3 months after you left
me I bought a 535 BMW, black and beautiful. I do

like everything about it, and I do thank you on this Valentine's Day—Feb. 14. I still have the red heart you gave me last year full of See's Candy Chocolates. Or was that a few years before? Oh God Jack, you see what I mean. It's all slipping away.

I would like to request a favor from you. Please be with me for I am very much in need of you, only you. Force your way through to me when I need you, please. I am lonely. I don't know why it was so hard for me to tell you how much I loved you when you were sitting across from me on the bar stool, drink in hand, music playing, dinner cooking, all things working? Maybe you know all the answers now that you've gone to the other side. I LOVE YOU JACK HALL.

Your Dorothy

Mom took care of Randy financially. He did not work. He continued to drink too much. He wrote, collaged, and saw his therapist, Dr. Markson, four times a week for fifteen-minute sessions.

On a visit to Randy's rental in Laguna Beach, where he'd moved after the Tangerine Street house, Dorrie recalls walking up the stairs to his unit over the garage. The place was, as expected, an all-too-familiar mess. When he asked her if she minded the way he kept spitting chewing tobacco into a glass filled with brown fluid, she shrugged. His clothes were grimy.

His skin was soft and flabby. In the middle of an awkward conversation about the possibilities of working at a bookstore, he walked out and didn't come back. But not before he'd shown her collages of women, their body parts cut from magazines and photographs.

The longer Randy lived, the more he became that Boo Radley character who lived down the street. The man the neighbors gossiped about in whispers . . . I imagined what they said: "Does he ever change those greasy clothes? What does he do all day?" "He doesn't even have a job." "He's always alone. Sometimes his mother or one of those sisters comes by. But that's it." "He never fixes that damn van he keeps parked on the street. It's an eyesore. And that smile, he always has that smile plastered over his face." "It's so weird. It's too weird. I keep my doors locked even in the day." Randy, the predator that never was.

At the beginning of filming *Something's Gotta Give*, I took little Dexter to meet her uncle. When the door opened, a bloated, gray-haired Randy, looking much older than fifty-four, missing a front tooth and sporting a long ponytail, ushered us in. As expected, a musky heaviness filled the air inside.

I was surprised when he took Dexter's hand, brought her to the kitchen area, and told her the secret of how he'd made his last night's meal. "Number one: put a chicken breast in a cup of orange juice inside a microwave. Number two: after zapping it to perfection, chop the orange-flavored chicken, add shiitake mushrooms, dill, salt, and pepper. Number three: introduce the lettuce last. It's delicious." Dexter stared, dumbstruck.

He went on to describe his routine of watching TV until

twelve noon every day. In the early afternoon, he'd hit one of several supermarkets he frequented, driving the old VW van. Once there, he'd stock up on the cheapest generic beer.

At some point in the conversation I asked Randy how he was doing.

"Living actually makes me sick sometimes. I tell you, Diane, I get emotional over the weirdest things. People's lives just kill me. It's strange. It's like we're living on a razor, and when we fall we split in half. I feel like I'm eight years behind with my anger."

As he rambled on, I couldn't help but think that, were it not for Mom's generous if ill-defined efforts, Randy would be on the street, abandoned, drunk, or even dead.

Still talking, he went on: "Recently, I've thought of suicide, but came to the conclusion that it's inherently wrong. It's better to hurt, because when you hurt you learn. I think I'm learning. I still believe a small, personal life can produce heroes."

I agreed. Taking Dexter's hand, I left Randy sitting inside his apartment drinking a beer, while watching Joseph Campbell and Bill Moyers discuss man and myth on PBS.

Mom called a few weeks later. "Diane, Randy came by in the van. Honest to goodness, I can't tell you what I thought. He did come here, didn't he?"

"I don't know, Mom; you tell me."

"I think he was here. Anyway, gosh, I hardly knew him. He's older. He looked a lot different. It's the age thing, the movement of time. I was so happy I went to bed in tears. I'd like to hear what he thought of me. He has the same laugh, and that same humor I love so much. But I have to tell you, I didn't recognize him at first."

Scattered and troubling conversations like this were beginning to become more and more frequent. She'd begun to leave open cans of Cyrus's unfinished cat food inside the kitchen cabinet. She'd drop her clothes on the floor and forget to pick them up. A couple teapots had to be replaced because she'd turn the burner on and forget it.

When she called about a visit to Randy's, I begrudgingly agreed to drive her. As he slowly opened the door, we were greeted by a pale phantom with a distended belly who didn't invite us in.

"Here's Mom, Randy."

His response was "Yeah."

Between the two of them, I didn't know what to do. Somehow, I managed to convince Randy to let us enter.

Soon after, I found myself filling out one of his insurance forms. "What's your Social Security number?" He didn't know. "Okay, don't worry about it. We'll get it later." Mom stood there, oblivious.

Later, as I held her hand walking down the stairs, she whispered, "He looks worse for the wear."

Several weeks later, Dorrie called to describe an afternoon she'd spent with Mom. "Of course, the only way to get her out of the house so her housekeeper could clean was to promise a visit to Randy. It broke my heart, how up for it she was. All I had to say was 'We're going to see Randy.' She burst into tears of joy, then promptly forgot. Once there, I noticed his hands shook, while she wandered around. He complained that his feet didn't work. She gave him her shoes. When I dropped her off, she took my hand in hers and said, 'Are you sure I live here, Dorrie? Are you sure I live here alone? Can't somebody come live here with me?'" After that, Dorrie, Robin, and I decided to take over all of Mom's affairs.

In February 2003, I was in the Hamptons with eight-year-old Dex and three-year-old Duke, taking a few days off from filming *Something's Gotta Give,* when Randy called and left a message on my answering machine. "Diane, I gotta get my car fixed. I'm waiting for the Triple A guy. Then I got to go to the DMV and get my license. But I feel dizzy. I get confused. The confusion is getting worse. I don't know. . . . I jumble things. I can't talk to people over the phone. I'm not eating a lot. I don't have the fat legs like I had before. Anyway, why doesn't this Triple A guy show up and get my car towed so I can get a battery?"

Dorrie drove down to his apartment, where he stood before her, looking like an apparition from a Grimm's fairy tale. He showed her the fluid that was oozing out of his stomach. Apparently, he'd taken a needle and pushed it into his belly button, figuring it was the only way to get the stuff out. He was hobbling like an old man. His shirt was drenched. His mattress was soaked. He wasn't making sense.

She told him to weigh himself. He came back and said he weighed eighty pounds. She told him it was impossible to weigh eighty pounds, and he should go back into the bathroom to try again.

When he came back, he said, "I weigh one eighty; that means without clothes I'd weigh one eighty-five."

In a panic, she drove him to nearby Mission Hospital in Laguna Beach, where they waited for hours in the emergency room. After they admitted him, the doctors told Dorrie that Randy's problem was not only the fluid that had built up as a result of his drinking, but also that the needle he'd pushed into his belly button to relieve the pain could have killed him.

With Robin in Atlanta and me still at work, Dorrie was left to bear the brunt of responsibility. I called Randy at Mission Hospital to hear how he was doing, and he did nothing but complain. "Before they threw me in the hospital, I went to Ralphs. I was leaking when the cashier said I had to leave. I was leaking all over the floor, Diane. They thought I was a drunk. Fuck them. I'm never going back there."

When I called Dorrie about his condition, she said she highly doubted he was up for the battle. He would have to pass a battery of tests, quit drinking, and apply himself to a rigorous routine. If Randy wanted to live, he was going to have to fight hard. But fighting had never been his preferred method of dealing with difficult situations.

A couple of weeks later, Robin and Dorrie called. Randy's lung had collapsed. The doctors at Mission felt our only chance was to try to get him evaluated at UCLA, where, if we were lucky, they might consider taking Randy as one of their patients. It was suggested that I personally get in touch; they felt it might be more effective.

But before I could do so, Dorrie called, sobbing, as Frida, my hairdresser, was blow-drying my hair. Randy had been diagnosed with end-stage cirrhosis of the liver. "Mom can't ever know, Diane. We can't ever tell her. It's too sad. Too sad. It's too sad." When she checked in with Dr. Markson, Randy's longtime psychiatrist, his response was "You didn't know? Randy never had a chance."

Feeling responsible, but also guilty, I called several surgeons at UCLA. After introducing myself as Randy Hall's sister, I gave them a highly revised version of his life. I talked of his artistry, his sensitivity, even a little bit about his drinking issues, which our family knew we could get under control with help. Their response seemed accommodating. Dorrie, Robin, and I were hopeful.

After three weeks in Paris and a brief stay in the Hamptons to complete filming of *Something's Gotta Give*, my on-location gypsy life was over. The movie was finished. Back in L.A., Dorrie and I were lucky enough to meet with a highly regarded surgeon at UCLA. "Randy is a very sick man," he said. "The problem is whether he'll be able to withstand the intense procedure required to receive a liver transplant." The conversation ended with a warning that, certainly, Randy could never drink again—not ever. We were grateful for his time, and reassured him that no, no, *of course* Randy would never drink again. It was painfully clear that a transplant was the only way to save his life.

That night, I dreamt my brother was walking down dark alleys, cutting deals with crooked men in black overcoats who were hoarding livers in briefcases to carry to various UCLA surgeons. The next day, we were told that Randy hadn't met the criteria for a transplant. The recommendations included: (1) six months of sobriety, (2) therapy, (3) documentation of the therapy, (4) continued psychiatric care. He would also need a re-evaluation to determine whether he was competent enough to undergo such a risky undertaking.

For UCLA to confirm Randy's worthiness to receive the rare gift of a liver transplant, we'd need two letters. The first had to come from Randy's day-to-day doctor in charge, the second, we hoped, from the doctor who would be assessing Randy. According to the assessor, because of Randy's record of extreme alcoholism, he would be required to complete the intensive Genesis Alcohol Rehab Program. But we knew Randy was wholly incapable of taking on that task.

Dorrie called Dr. Markson, who wrote a letter to the head of the liver-transplant department at UCLA, asking if Randy could be given the opportunity for a new beginning, even though it was alcohol consumption that had caused his lethal cirrhosis of the liver. Dr. Markson described Randy as a highly imaginative artist who had a good heart and many continuing gifts to share with the world. Without this doctor's help, I doubt Randy would be alive.

In addition to Dr. Markson, our father, the man who'd toiled his way to success, came back from the dead to save the day. One day later, Mom's accountant, Terry Ward, sent a large check as a contribution to the Department of Surgery, Liver and Pancreas Transplant Division, at UCLA. Soon after, Randy was secured a place on the list. Jack Hall, his mound of ashes scattered on a rock pile underneath a wooden cross in

Tubac, Arizona, bequeathed Randy his transplant number. It was thirty-eight.

I never questioned whether his inclusion on the list was justified. I conveniently avoided pondering the morality of why he was chosen over someone who was more deserving but couldn't write such a check. He was my brother. The experience—the way it played itself out, the all-too-familiar, painfully sad choices that brought Randy to UCLA—was overwhelming. As Randy waited to be reborn, I wondered if he had it in him—morally, physically, spiritually, emotionally, even genetically—to be a grateful recipient of a second-chance gift of life.

I'll never forget the day I found him lying on a bed in Room 601, which he shared with three other failing liver patients. There was one Mr. Avery, Edward, and an older Vietnamese gentleman whose bed was by the window. Randy, nearest the door, had pressing reports from the field: "I had a total relapse. Last night, everyone started turning into paintings. They had fangs—I'm telling you the truth."

In the middle of his next sentence, one of the nurses walked in, handed me a menu, and told me to figure out what John Randolph wanted for his next three meals, because she was tired of putting an "X" for him beside coffee, grape juice, pasta with marinara, Cheerios, scrambled eggs, and pudding. She said he didn't have a clue what he liked, and he never cooperated.

Without pausing, Randy interjected: "There are so many fucked-up people around here. It's always this way. You can't change a thing. Maybe it's for the best. I don't know. It's hard to tell."

As the nurse handed me his iced tea, she insisted I at least try to make him understand that he was in a hospital. Randy took a sip, then threw back the covers, revealing his bone-thin purple arms and yellow fingers. "Diane, could you loan me five dollars?"

Suddenly a loud voice over the intercom called for backup, while a nurse shouted, "Mr. Avery, are you all right?" An attendant rushed over to a neighboring bed and screamed, "Mr. Avery, we need to get you oxygen."

Randy, ignoring the fuss, said, "I'd like to go home, Diane. Even if I don't get well, I'd like to go home."

Days later, at 8:25 a.m. on July 25, 2003, I got the call from Randy's doctor. "I've got a liver for your brother, John. We're going to be transplanting him today at noon."

When Dorrie and I walked into Room 601, an almost skeletal Randy looked at us and said: "This is a great day. I'll be able to go to therapy. I'll walk. I'll play my guitar. I'll do my collages and get back to writing." Dorrie and I gave him a big kiss. Robin called to send her love. The three of us decided to help keep Mom free from worry by hiding the full truth of Randy's condition and operation. When Randy looked at his reflection in the TV on the wall, he laughed and said, "Geez, I'm an old fart. I hope the surgeon doesn't do anything stupid. Don't forget, after they close the curtain, we can go to the movies. We'll be able to see *Seabiscuit* with Tobey Maguire."

That night, Robin, Dorrie, and I got messages from the

surgeon. Mine said: "Hi, Diane, how are you? I just wanted to give you a follow-up. It's about ten-thirty on Friday night. I just left Randy from the ICU. He looks terrific. Hopefully, we'll get the tube out, probably in the morning, and the liver's working great. Everything's going super."

The intensive-care unit was like being in a full-service 24-7 city of last chance. When I spotted Randy, looking pink, with clear eyes, I wondered why he wasn't semi-comatose and groaning in pain after seven hours under the knife. Later, I learned he was on steroids.

Almost immediately, he started in with one of his monologues. "So it worked. I've got a liver, and it's a dandy. Did you know Danny DeVito's here? I hear he's going to rally. I sure could use a drink. Nurse, you don't happen to have a cup of water, do you?"

The nurse, who handed me a swab of water on a green sponge that looked like a Popsicle, said, "He's a real character, your brother. He's doing well, very, very well."

In the middle of his steroid-infused monologue, Randy went on: "She undid my legs; the only trouble is, I can't walk. The damn nurse undid my legs, Diane. Man, I wish I had more water. I don't know where my stilts are. Have you seen them?"

After several weeks, Randy began getting prepped to be released. There was the lesson on how to use the commode, the oxygen tank, the wheelchair, and even the walker. Dorrie and I were ushered into the belly of the medical center to have our own lessons on physical therapy.

We began to notice that the better he got, the more he became the same old Randy. Dorrie begged him to cut his nails—the same nails the surgeon had warned him about. Randy chose to inform the doctor who'd saved his life that he was the tenth idiot to give directions he had no intention of following. The surgeon responded, "Yes, but I'm your doctor." At least Randy had the smarts to stay silent as he looked up at the TV set to watch Stanley Holloway in *My Fair Lady* sing and dance his way through "With a Little Bit of Luck."

My friend Carol Kane let us rent her California bungalow just off Sunset Boulevard for Randy while he recovered. Robin recommended we hire a nurse named Treena to look after him, a no-nonsense gal with a great sense of humor. Dorrie and I trusted her implicitly.

In an effort to help Randy make good choices with his new life, Dorrie and I decided to schedule a meeting with Dr. Markson to see if he could give us more advice. He graciously agreed. We were taken aback by his concern.

"I told your brother that when he got to the hospital he needed to call me. You know what he did? Two weeks later, he finally called and said, 'Help,' then hung up. That's Randy. Look, I couldn't get him to go to the store to buy a pair of pants. If his DVD player was broken, I'd say, 'Bring in the DVD player—we can figure it out.' How many times did he bring it in? None. None.

"Let's face it, the major thing with Randy is, he needs space between him and other people. If that space is easy, it's okay.

If there are demands, he can't take it. When he was writing, he didn't want people to read his work. He needed an editor. I wanted to enhance his socialization, but he took criticism very badly. If someone asks him a question, and he can't answer it, it fills him with panic. If challenged, he can't even get into a car, 'cause he's afraid someone might ask him a question and he'd shut down. One question and he collapses. 'What are they asking? How can I answer?' He does have a real thirst for knowledge. He thinks his work is terrible. He'd bring in a collage. I'd get some meaning from it. He'd say, 'That's interesting,' and that was it. He was finished. He didn't talk about it again.

"Toward the end, he'd come in here filled up with fluid, and more fluid. I told him dying of a corroded liver is a terrible way to go. It's amazing how that early problem of being pushed around by your father has never been resolved. He used to say he lived in a metal sphere orbiting the earth. That was his fantasy, to be completely protected. We have to know when to stop pushing. He's so self-destructive. He's deprived himself of so much. He's suicidal. He doesn't talk about it, but he thinks about it. He talks about being helpless."

Dr. Markson ended our session with these words: "You have to continue to be gently supportive, but also know when to stop pushing. As I've said, he has a real thirst for knowledge. Look, my advice is . . . forget about hygiene. Just concentrate on three basic things with Randy: one, no drinking; two, take pills; three, see doctors on a regular basis."

Was there a name for Randy's mental illness, if that's what it was? In later years, one doctor described Randy as a schizoid personality—i.e., emotionally cold, detached, apathetic. I don't remember Randy as apathetic or cold. I do remember it was hard to understand what was going on with him. If there was a problem, if he was under pressure, if a situation called for him to step up and be a man, Randy consistently refused to take arms. Yet his fantasies were the exact opposite of his actions. In his fantasies, he was a warrior, even a murderer. How do you explain that?

In his early twenties, some of those fantasies began to make their way to written expression as he sat on his favorite yellow chair and wrote down sentences like "I like to think of Time as a joke no one can hear." Or "Learning how to love is slow, like molasses. I doubt I'll ever find its foot prints in the dust of my attempts." "I do not want to be born again. Once is enough. Why would I want to feel this sadness for a second time?" "Give me whatever death is. It can be nothing but comfort after years of twisted feelings that can't be explained, only endured." "I love this room where I sit in my yellow chair and purge. If I wait long enough it feeds me fairytales. I pull them from the darkness I wandered in when I was a little boy."

Looking back on Randy's symptoms has been like opening up an old crime-scene investigation. I asked myself again and again: *Was I guilty?* Or, rather, how guilty was I? Searching for clues has been a losing enterprise. When I've tried to assemble Randy's past into a cohesive explanation for his so-called indifference, I get sidetracked; I can't quite place the events or the details.

Markson wasn't wrong about aspects of our brother's condition, but Randy was not apathetic. Fearful, yes. But not indifferent. Pinpointing a mental illness is like finding a needle in a haystack. I wouldn't want to be part of a team that labels the most complex organ of our body with a name. Randy was not a category, and medicine is not an exact science. Part of his saving grace came from the outlet he found in expression, whether it was seemingly negative—visualizing women in sadomasochistic positions—or something aiming for transcendence: writing lyrical poems on the wonder of birds. Yes, he explored the dark side, but he also wrote:

All the voices of my past are here tonight in this grassy clearing at the foot of the mountains, where I came to sleep. At first I thought it was the rattle of nesting birds, perhaps rocks falling from a cliff. But, like bells, the words took shape. Paragraphs echoed out of trees. Stories of other lives hung sadly in the air like pages of failure. I did not want to listen, until I heard my own voice high on the flat face of the mountains. I heard it barely stumbling over the meadows. I heard it echoing out of the trees, one more sad voice, I heard my story reverberating in the air along with the other voices of failure at the foot of the mountains where I came to sleep.

Once he was settled in Carol Kane's bungalow, the problems began to rear their ugly heads in a small, progressive, yet persistent series of events. Nurse Treena reprimanded Randy for eating too many protein bars. She insisted on cutting his fingernails. She was on him to take the pills the doctors had prescribed. She didn't want him smoking cigars. After a couple days off, Treena came back to find him smoking cigars with the fill-in nurse, Ophelia. She was not happy. Randy didn't appreciate her concern. He didn't want some "Bible-toting woman" bossing him around. He also didn't want his sisters harping at him about the necessity of reading the red pamphlet his transplant coordinator had given him weeks before. He didn't care how important it was to understand what the pills did and why he should adhere to a strict regimen in order to stay healthy. As Randy began to walk on his own, he discovered the ATM up the block. And that's when he started buying beer from the 7-Eleven across the street.

I was in New York, in a car heading uptown—I'd just finished a joint interview with Gus Van Sant on the *Today* show for the movie *Elephant,* which he'd directed and I'd been a producer on—when I got a call from Dorrie. "Treena, the nurse, found an empty tequila bottle next to Randy's bed."

Poor Dorrie. She'd had it. Although she'd reminded him how much he needed Treena, he went so far as to tell her, in no uncertain terms, that Treena was out. He wanted Ophelia to come three times a week to check in, buy some groceries, and take him to the hospital on Mondays and Thursdays. Dorrie, knowing full well Randy didn't know what pills to take and when, expressed concern about his readiness for independence. Randy began screaming, saying Treena was a controlling bitch, and hung up.

What could we do? Treena quit, and Ophelia continued

as a sometime check-in nurse. I called him from New York, leaving a benign message. I called again and again. There was no response.

Randy's insistent refusal to take even the slightest responsibility for himself drove Dorrie crazy. I couldn't blame her. Robin and I weren't there to help. "He doesn't think of the implications, Diane. He was on his way out. Is he grateful in any way other than a general nod of appreciation in our direction? Does he know the names of the twenty-five pills he has to take daily? Does he read the booklet his transplant co-coordinator gave him? Has he memorized the phone numbers of his lifeline? Does he clean himself? Has he written anything? Is he a writer? Does he address the huge financial expenditure that has been made on his behalf? Does he even worry? Does he think about his future as he watches *E! Hollywood* and *True Story*? Yesterday he asked me if I knew who really killed Thelma Todd. Thelma Todd!!!!! Some twenties party-girl actress? A day isn't a day without *Access Hollywood*?"

Weeks later, when I was finally back home, Dorrie and I found Randy sitting under a pepper tree drinking a quart of Cuervo Gold tequila in Carol Kane's front yard. As we approached, Dorrie spoke first. "How are you doing?"

"I knew you two would come by. I wondered how long it would take."

"We're concerned about you, Randy."

"Fuck you. You dress like a couple of dykes. Fuck you both. I don't give a rat's ass about anybody. I hate people. I don't want to live. Why should I?" As he spun around, he grabbed his bottle, went inside, and slammed the door. Dorrie and I followed as his stammering outburst continued. "See these teeth? Yes, they're rotten, I know. Do you think I'm an idiot? No. You never listened to me."

Dorrie interrupted. "We want to listen now."

"Fuck you. And fuck you too, Diane."

I tried to take the bottle out of his hand, saying some stupid thing, like "Randy, we need to take you to the hospital."

He began swirling it as if he was going to throw it at us. "Leave me alone. I don't want your help," he shouted, his eyes defiant. We called the paramedics.

After Randy was admitted to the lockdown wing of the Ronald Reagan UCLA Medical Center, I called him. He hung up when he heard my voice. A few weeks later, while I was getting Dexter ready for school, the hospital called; my brother, John, wanted to talk to me. A sober Randy got on.

"I want you to come here and take me to Laguna. I want to go home and drink."

"I can't do that, Randy."

"Why not? Don't you want to help me do what I want to do with my life?"

"Yes."

"Then let me live it the way I want and stop interfering."

"Yes, Randy, it is your life, but you made a deal. You wanted the transplant. It was your decision. A dying man gave it to you. Did you ever consider that??? He gave it to you instead of someone else. You're alive because of him and his anonymous generosity. You owe him."

Randy shot back, "I was waiting for you to say that. Let me tell you something. . . . I never wanted this, ever, and I don't owe anybody anything."

I immediately called Robin, who, as a former nurse, had a better way of handling Randy's moods. When she called back, her advice was to let him go. It was his life, and his decision.

A week later, in October of 2003, I picked up the phone to hear: "Hello, Diane. Come and get me, 'cause they're going to let me out. I want to go to Laguna Beach. I'm not going back to Carol Kane's. I've never felt better in my life. I've never felt more free. I'm an alcoholic. And I don't care. Just get me out of here. Don't mess with me. I've been screwed twenty million times since I've been here. I will never stop drinking, ever. Come and take me home. It's my body. Just say yes and drive me home. I want to live on my own terms. These holier-than-thou doctors are nothing but Bible thumpers. I don't like people. The only thing I like is my writing and my art. Don't bother with me, Diane. Okay? Just take me home. Please."

I did.

CHAPTER 10

SLIPPING AWAY

In 1998, Mom had been formally diagnosed with early-onset Alzheimer's disease. Even though she admitted she was having trouble with her ability to recall names and events, she vowed she would overcome her memory issues. But, following her decline, Robin flew in and helped us hire Ann Mayer, who would become Mom's assistant. Ann in turn gathered together Susie Dionisio and Irma Flores, a couple of wonderful women, to care for her. Randy, on the other hand, wasn't interested in Mom's state of mind. His wish was to be left alone. We honored the request.

Dorrie called: "Mom is freezing Pablo and J.C.'s cat food. I found two tea bags next to several loaves of molded country white bread in the freezer. She's fine, she says, as she wanders around the house holding on to the walls. She can't get her balance. She doesn't remember to drink lots of water. She doesn't remember to prepare food. She doesn't want to see me. She doesn't want to play Scrabble or take walks on the beach. What she is, is quietly struggling on the perimeter of thoughts that won't express themselves.

"I see she's hiding what she can't remember. She's afraid to drive to Los Angeles. She's afraid of falling. She's seventy-seven. It's a hodgepodge mess. Random books line the back wall, next to dozens of collages by Randy, including a metal roadrunner I bought her in Tubac. There's a new look in the living room: sterility. It's like Mom is disappearing. She's beginning to let go."

Later, I got a call from Mom herself. "Oh God, Diane, I'm awful. I'm not doing good. People are over here. I don't know how to focus, Diane. I don't trust my walk. I get up in the morning with the intention of doing things, but then I can't remember. I don't go anywhere. I don't want to do anything. It's terrible. Just wait until you're old."

Years later, breaking a long silence, I finally called Randy and told him he needed to visit his mother. After all, he was the love of her life. I'd drive him there—anything. He said he was busy working on some new collages and writing at night. I asked if he had any feelings for her distressing situation. He said if he did he would have mentioned it. I told him how much she missed him. Randy was silent on the other end of the line. I was still waiting for a response when I got a call from someone else, and took it.

On New Year's Day, after a visit with Mom, I forced myself to drive to the apartment off the Pacific Coast Highway where Randy had been living. He opened the door. A gangsta-style beanie was pulled over his forehead. His white beard touched his chest. As expected, he was wearing a greasy sweatshirt, and he shook. His hands shook. His head shook. His whole body shook. When we sat down, I looked at the filthy floor in front of the love seat he slept on. The Monterey coffee table I'd given him years before was piled high with photographs, paint, brushes, and hundreds of magazines. The entire room was a gallery of collages he'd Scotch Taped, hammered, and glued to the walls. They also lined the floor, in stacks that reached the ceiling. As in the old Tangerine Street days, he even stored them inside his oven. Coffee cups filled with chewing tobacco rested on the arm of every chair. When I took note of a pink background framing a woman whose eyes had become pins, her mouth spewing out hypodermic needles, I could see clearly that he took the art of collaging very far.

As he picked up several spiral-bound notebooks, I reminded myself I was there to check in, listen to some of his poems, and above all to persuade him to visit our ailing mother. He sat down with a beer in hand and read:

"Today there is nothing in the sky. It is easy to imagine myself spread like blue enamel above the earth. Easy too are the winds that wash my hands, and stir my fantasies." Listening, I began to imagine how it might feel to be spread like blue enamel above the earth. For a moment, I let go of my duty to Mom, and thought about Randy's use of words. Endless words. He read a poem he calls "Bits and Pieces":

"My yellow chair is a living thing. It feeds me fairy tales. My chair pulls me away from the darkness I wandered in when I was young. My life was the nightmare I hid my dreams from."

For Randy, words were up for grabs, playthings, a form of diversion utilized in an atmosphere filled with meaning and emotion.

Joining Randy with a beer, I wondered how a six-foot-two-inch man could sleep on a love seat and be comfortable in such a filthy mess. Once more, I asked him to go see Mom, promising to drive him there and back.

He smiled. "Did I ever tell you about the lawn-mowing thing? I was thirteen or fourteen. We lived on Wright Street. I'd been given a job. Every week, I'd mow the lawn. When I was done, Mom would come out and re-mow it because I did such a lousy job. She couldn't stop herself. She did that kind of thing all the time. Why was I mowing the lawn if she was going to do it over again?"

He paused. "Mom was a sweetheart—she'd just gotten in with a weird guy. She did have her moods, though. Remember how she'd boil up inside when Laurel Bastendorf would drop over for coffee and a talk? Remember how she'd complain about how Laurel would never shut up? People bored Mom. Who does that sound like? Me, I know. I hate it when people talk too much."

How had Randy come to find himself sitting in a rental on the wrong side of the Pacific Coast Highway, bordering on old age? How had I, the eldest of four Southern California kids who grew up in the 1950s, become an ambitious eccentric who couldn't stop worrying? There was something about Randy's traipsing around his apartment that reminded me to try to let go. No matter how truncated and seemingly lost, Randy was fine, living his life with a mind let loose. Sitting across from him, I thought: There is no scale tipped in either direction that can measure the worth of one person over another. All of us are, as Randy put it best, "a blink between here and never."

Looking back, when I try to reconstruct the past into a cohesive explanation for Randy's indifference, his lack of gratitude—especially toward powerful men, including the doctors at UCLA, not to mention the liver donor, who gave him another twenty to thirty years of life—I get confused. Perhaps it has something to do with his total disregard for reality.

As I sat there, I wondered if his writing's principal purpose was to soothe. Once again, he said it best: "I have no need to be known for the words I put to paper like food to an empty mouth longing to explain a life unknown." Then I thought: If you're Randy, and you've lived your whole life hiding clandestine fantasies, yet you haven't let your impulses fully realize them, like Dennis Hastert, the former wrestling coach who allegedly had sex with an underage male student, or Jerry Sandusky, a convicted child molester who had been assistant coach at Penn State University, what does that say? How about Josh Duggar, the Christian reality-show star who was accused of having sex with one of his sisters and other young girls, even though he paraded around as a role model for the stellar Christian family man? All three of these so-called good men acted out their fantasies, then hid their crimes. All were accomplished, their public records a glowing example. Yet Randy, a semi-homeless-looking man who didn't comply with normalcy, was guilty of nothing. Not only that, Randy never lied about who he was. Even to himself, about his fantasy life. He once wrote me a letter describing the role fantasy played for him.

Dear Diane,

In puberty I started getting into fantasies. They were pretty innocent in the beginning, but they progressively got more graphic. I became addicted to watching horror movies, hoping the films would have some gruesome murder of a woman. I saw one that made an impression. It was called *The Zodiac Killer*. A man stabs this woman with a switchblade. He continues stabbing her as she screams. Screaming became my idea of heaven. My fantasies began to focus on the concept of stabbing mannequins because it would be more effective and they were more human than watching a movie. Mannequins have breasts. As my fantasies progressed they got pretty messy. I'll never forget the day I found the *Playboy* magazine hidden in some bushes in a field. I looked inside and saw a woman with all this cleavage leaning against a fence. I took it home and kept it under my bed. Of course, guess who saw them? Yeah you. At that time, you were somewhat of a fink. When you showed the pictures to mom I was horrified. I didn't want to tell her I was whacking myself. I hated getting caught, mainly because the fantasies were startling, and violent. When I thought about sex it was always with a knife. It had to be a knife, you know; the phallic symbol. My dick. You can't imagine what it's like to actually start planning how to get a pretty woman and kill her. I did Diane, I had scenarios of doing just that. I figured I would sneak into a room where a woman was sleeping and stab her to death. My fantasies are even worse now, but at least I know they're fantasies. I'm not going to do anything. I never wanted normal women. All I could think about was sexy women. They had all the stuff I wanted to get a hold of. If I couldn't have them at least I could kill them. It got really weird. But I have to say, holding it back all those years makes me believe I am a moral man. James Ellroy used to break into houses and steal underwear. I can't even do that. I can't even break into a house and steal underwear. I couldn't, but boy could I dream of it.

Love, Randy

Randy's confession came to me just after I had finished shooting *Reds,* in Europe. As disturbing and unexpected as the letter was, I trusted what he said and chose not to show it to anyone—not even Robin and Dorrie. Until now. I felt he had a right to his fantasies. After all, I was someone who played parts, living out fantasies in the safe realm of movies.

CHAPTER 11

SURRENDERING TO
THE RUSH OF WINGS

In David Shenk's book on Alzheimer's, *The Forgetting,* he quotes Morris Friedell, who died from the disease. Alzheimer's is "the best lens on the meaning of loss," but it's also a condition that "acquaints us with life's richness by ever so gradually drawing down the curtains."

This was true for Dorothy, who in the last throes of Alzheimer's became a haunting shadow of her former self. By this point, she had round-the-clock hospice care at home. Robin, Dorrie, and I continued to prod Randy into making a visit. In 2008, when it looked like there wasn't much time left, he finally was forced to show up.

As he sat on the edge of her hospital bed in the living room overlooking the ocean, we recorded him saying: "Mom, this is your idiot son. Do you remember when Dorrie, Robin, you, and I were driving the car across country? Remember the Ford Econoline van? We were all going to New York to visit Diane. Remember when we spent the night at that crazy lady's place in New Jersey? It was a real dump. She had that blind Chihuahua named Rickie Lee. She was one weird piece of work, but she loved that Rickie Lee. Remember how she kissed that slobbering thing? Do you? Do you remember any of that?

"New York was quite a place. We went to the Museum of Modern Art, where we saw the Jasper Johns, Picassos, Turners, but most of all those Joseph Cornell boxes—remember? I'm sure you do. Come on, Mom. Give me a wink, just a little wink. You know I'm here, don't you? Yeah, you do! You're chirping—see, you're chirping! Come on! Wake up! Get up. Get up and at 'em.

"Hey, Mom, I want you to know that I'm living in the best place in the world. I wouldn't have it any other way. I hope to live there till I die. I finally get to do what I want to do. I'm still writing, and collaging. Hey, you should come see my house now. There's a little living room with a kitchen, and a bedroom and bathroom."

He kissed her, and that was it. Randy never saw her again.

Mom did not die as expected. She lingered. After a few weeks, Robin, who'd flown in from Georgia, had to go home to Riley, Jack, and her husband, Rickey. Dorrie and I came down on weekends to spend the nights at the house with her. One month later, we got a call from Mom's primary caregiver, Ann Mayer: "Come soon." She was near the end.

On the night Mom passed, Dorrie, Robin, and I were with her. After the purple-draped Mom was rolled into a van on a gurney in one of her go-to-dinner outfits, I woke up knowing there would never be another person who would love and care for us Hall kids the way she had. I was going to have to rely on myself. I would never again watch her fry up homemade tacos, or take a walk on the beach, or collect seashells, or feed her crippled seagull before sitting down to hear one of my sad stories of being misunderstood in an unfair situation. She was my once-in-a-lifetime compassionate listener.

Dexter and Duke wanted to know why Gramma had to die. I told them Grammie's heart had slowed down, her circulation was weak, her hands began to look like beautiful purple plums, and then, without a hint, she quietly stopped breathing. I told them she had left to go on a special journey into an unknown wonderland.

On the drive to Mom's memorial service at Casa Romantica in San Clemente, I turned the radio up to hear a woman's voice. In a clipped British accent, she was saying her father had a birdhouse where he kept white doves. Every morning, he would get up early and care for the doves. When World War II came, it changed their lives. There was always a peaceful, quiet quality in the air before the bombing began. People stayed in their homes. They were told not to go out. Despite this, her father still went to the doves every morning. One day, she wanted to go to work with him, but he told her to stay in the house. She watched him walk off in the early-morning light. Fifteen minutes later, the bombs came. Suddenly big men came looking for her mother. They found her at the bakery. She remembers her mother sobbing. She remembers her sinking to the ground in a river of tears. On the day of her father's funeral, her mother went to the birdhouse and let the doves go, one by one. The girl didn't understand: why did her mother let the birds her father loved so go? Her mother said, "I had to let your father go. Now I am letting them go too." At the funeral procession, friends and family carried her father's casket to his burial ground. And the birds, all of them, followed the casket in their own winged procession to his resting place.

That's what Mom's memorial felt like. It felt like we were the birds she'd taken care of, and even though we couldn't fly, we were following her to her resting place. Randy led the way.

When I dropped by Randy's a few months later, I asked him if he ever thought about Mom.

"Yeah, I do. It's hard for me to picture her dead."

"When you do, what do you see?" I asked.

"I see the end years, when her hair was really white," he said. And then, "I don't know, there was something about her. I really never knew much about Mom, not really. I wish I did, but I didn't."

For Randy, arranging brutal words into poetry may have been a way to explore his anger, and his self-hatred. In his darkest hours, maybe he used some of his poems as confessional mirrors—places where he felt safe to confront and even forgive himself for his sadistic urges; places where he explored murder, mayhem, and sexual brutality. In such a place, he also wrote about Mom.

> *I am my mother's Homunculus;*
> *a little girl with a penis,*
> *running about on clawed feet,*
> *lost to the alchemy of love and emotion,*
> *a bastard thing she chose not to see or hear*
> *or take in hand and lead to an acceptable life.*

What do I know about her?
She had a strict, religious upbringing,
her father walked out the door when she was sixteen
later a car accident mangled her inner thigh,
and her mother hated men.
She did not release this information (as little as it is)
until she had enough wine to relax the demons,
her face would soften,
her speech became fluid, her eyes moist.
Out came torn up pieces of her history.
They didn't always fit and were never explained.
I got the picture of a fragmented woman
trying to fill in the spaces with her own family,
a loving woman who couldn't quite love,
a caring mother who was never cared for.
If today were my last day on this planet
I would have one wish;
To be inside my mother's head for an hour.
God the pain and freedom of knowing the core
of one who created me,
kind of like seeing my own future.
But today is not my last day
and human secrets are deep and terrifying.
It is my job to figure out the rest of my life without her.
It will be a maze lacking a center.
But there is satisfaction in testing new paths.
I can learn where I begin and mother ends—

CHAPTER 12

HILLARY

When Randy first began knocking on his Laguna Beach neighbors' doors, asking them to please take him home, they were sweet and concerned, and responded with kindness. When it became a nightly routine, the police were called. They kindly drove him home. One night, Randy had a big fall. An ambulance drove him to Mission Hospital Laguna Beach, where the diagnosis included a small stroke, but the treatment seemed more like a plan for long-term-care solutions related to dementia. We transferred him to the UCLA Medical Center.

Dorrie and I sat with the neurologist, in his office at UCLA. "Randy's doing well with eating and drinking. Since the two weeks he's been at the center, he's settled in. His memory is a little better. He's done pretty well with counting, especially counting backwards. He's not going to get all his memory back. Let me put it this way. . . . If he had a twenty-dollar bill for the purchase of a six-pack of beer, he wouldn't be able to figure out how much change he'd get in return. The

MRI shows evidence of a narrowing of the blood vessels from alcohol abuse. It's hard to define what kind of dementia he has. There are patterns that have taken a toll on his brain. If his dementia is only related to alcohol use, there's a possibility it could go away. But when he was tested, the deficits were significant, especially with memory. He may only recover slightly. In the end . . . he shouldn't be by himself. With that in mind, he needs to be closely supervised. He needs consistency. He has tremors. He's imbalanced. We're not saying he has the beginning of Alzheimer's, but we're starting him on Aricept."

After Randy was discharged, Dorrie and I were given another list: (1) he should not take Ativan; (2) he can't drink ever again; (3) he should take Lipitor; (4) take one aspirin a day for stroke prevention; (5) he can't live alone; (6) assisted living would work best. Whether he likes it or not, he needs people. People are therapeutic.

The Belmont Village Senior Living facility, located at 455 East Angeleno Avenue, was within walking distance of downtown Burbank. Standing four stories high on a residential street, Belmont had a sense of community. The apartments were light, even airy. When Dorrie and I told the manager Randy was an artist, he ushered us into a one-bedroom apartment on the third floor with a friendly-looking work space framed by a large picture window, where Randy could collage and write. We took it on the spot.

Downstairs, we saw residents eating lunch. The ladies were dressed up, and the men seemed to accept the formality. Belmont's dining room didn't smell like some of the ones Dorrie and I had encountered in other assisted-living facilities. Out of the corner of my eye, I noticed a pool table and a popcorn machine in the activities room. We'd made the right decision.

In the years Randy lived at Belmont, he participated in more socializing and had more crushes and more friends than he'd experienced in his lifetime. Best of all, he had that light-filled apartment, enhanced with a long, durable work table that Dorrie and I bought at Ikea. Outside his window was an old sycamore tree. In the eight-hundred-square-foot, three-room apartment, he listened to music, ate, wrote, cut up portraits of blond-haired women with hot red lips, and pasted them on canvases he bought at the art-supplies store. We hired a young caregiver named Hillary McFarland, who was full of ideas. She single-handedly reinvigorated him with a mountain of projects, doctors' visits, and friendship—real friendship.

Since Randy was a lot younger than the other residents, he took on the role of a cool-cat James Dean outsider who'd dropped in on parties. He even created his own special style of gliding some lucky woman around the floor. The ladies adored him.

In an e-mail to me describing this time, Hillary wrote:

Randy's feeling great about himself. He looks at things like he's seeing them for the first time. He loves to go on walks. I asked him how come he likes to walk so far. He said because he doesn't think about where he's going. We usually start off with no destination in mind; just walk to walk. Without a goal he feels free. Maybe that's why he enjoys it so much. Randy loves texture. He'll stop and feel the trunk of a tree. He'll pick up leaves just to touch them; to marvel at their size, their color. They say one of the qualities of dementia is a hoarding or collecting behavior. Randy's started collecting gum wrappers, rocks, coke bottles, and even an abandoned baby sock. What looks like trash to me is art to him. All of these odd collectibles have brought him happiness. He's seeing things he's never seen before; feeling things he's never felt before. This is probably one of his best times, in that he's been given the gift of not remembering the debilitating past.

He loves chewing gum. He puts his chewed pieces on the lamp base next to his bed to save for later. As sure as hell, I've caught him grabbing a week-old piece of gum, popping it in his mouth and starting to chew it again! A few weeks ago, he started complaining that he was going deaf. Off to the doctor we went. The nurse flushed his ears with warm saline and alcohol rinse, then got a tool and pulled out these big black chunks of earwax and dirt. Suddenly he could hear again. The doctor had to remind him to cut his nails. The dirt underneath could cause an infection, so I started giving him manicures. At first, he resisted, but eventually he liked them. A lot.

Randy's time at Belmont has brought him out of his hermit state. He's learned to tolerate people in small groups. Once, I accompanied him to the dining room to try and help him socialize over a meal. That didn't go over well. He likes bingo though. Just a couple of months ago he came back from one of his walks and sat down with a resident who was playing Kings in The Corner. He began playing with her. She's 97 years old! Every time he joins her, she has to teach him to play the game over again. One day, she asked him what her name was. He said he didn't know, she shook her head, "You sit here and play cards with me all the time, you're young enough to be my grandson, and you don't know my name?" He said, "No, I don't, but I'll play cards with you anyway." Sometimes he just sits and watches her play. I think he feels comfortable just being around her. Maybe she reminds him of his mother.

As the youngest one in the joint, Randy's begun playing some serious pool. He's taught me a lot of pointers and I've gotten pretty good at some shots. Now, when men come to visit their family members, they look for Randy to shoot a game. His favorite saying for missing a shot is "I screwed the pooch." He can curse with the best of them. Sometimes he yells "fucking shit," and has to be calmed down. I've seen him take his hat off and throw it across the table after a lousy shot.

We've been on some great adventures, like driving to the beach, and putting our feet in the sand. We visited the LA Zoo in Griffith Park. We saw the Autry Museum, and the Observatory, too. We went to the

Natural History Museum, LACMA, MOCA, The La Brea Tar Pits, Watts Towers, The Getty, the Adamson House, and the Manhattan Beach Pier. We've ridden the Metro from North Hollywood to Union Station and walked to Philippe's for lunch. Randy cracked me up when he tried to convince me we were in New York riding the subway. He marveled at how we got to New York so fast! I loved seeing the wonder in his eyes. He really relishes going on an adventure.

All the Best,

Hillary

Randy fell in love with Hillary. One of the poems he wrote at Belmont is titled "Lady H.":

I like the nature of Hillary, her forward Ho! Lady H. is my Island. I sail in her direction. Hell-o my cur-vaceous colors of a rainbow. I only hope my words touch her essence and speak gently. She is harmony in every move she makes. I want to waltz in her shadow, humming like a comet between the open spaces of unknown planets.

CHAPTER 13

FOSTER'S FREEZE

Randy and I began to develop a weekend ritual. Down the block and across the street from Belmont was a Foster's Freeze, home to our very favorite soft-serve vanilla cone with nuts on top. Once we had them in our hands, we'd get into my car and tool around Burbank, looking for a neighborhood we wanted to explore. Much to my surprise, Randy would often lead the way. "You know, my work has gotten better, Diane, mainly because I've been forced to deal with people. Before, I was in my own one-sided world. Now I'm seeing the other side. Whether I like Belmont or not, I'm learning."

One Sunday, we passed a church where people were exiting in their Sunday best. Randy hated the suits and ties, which he was sure the men had been forced to wear. "You want to know what I believe, Diane? Here's what I believe: I believe God exists in human art. I believe in our struggle to explain what can't be explained. I believe people are the essence of beauty brought together by wonder. Living in itself is an act of courage."

Sometimes, after I parked the car to drop him off, he'd have me come in so he could read one of his recent pieces. "I always thought I would love sitting on a hill overlooking the vast meadow of God's best creations. I was certain my poetry would take great leaps forward. It didn't happen, thanks to God's distractions. Here's my question to Mr. God: Who will bleach the stars when the heavens go black? Who will wash my socks on the day I die?"

On one Foster's Freeze outing, we were surprised by a house at Olive Avenue and Ninth Street. Randy wanted to get out of the car and walk around the stone-covered California bungalow, built with what must have been tons of indigenous river rock. According to him, the cozy landmark was a scientific venture into new building practices. As he rambled on, another subject came to mind. "You know, I read about these scientists who worked twenty years in an attempt to find a sign of Pluto, even though there wasn't any. When they finally found it, no one believed them. They'd spent all those years looking for a planet the size of a sharpened pencil. How could anyone dedicate their lives in search of something that abstract?"

Those weekends of looking without an agenda gave me a glimpse into the wonder of Randy's imagination. Welcoming every direction on impulse led us in and out of the perimeters of Burbank. Being with him helped me let go of old habits and tired routines. For the first time in years, I began to take in his face. I noticed it was getting better with age, just like Mom's. Maybe their beauty had been enhanced by the pain they endured, or the depth of their feeling—I don't know. I do know this: Randy was giving me a path to new perceptions.

One day, about to cruise through a new neighborhood after we'd finished our vanilla cones, Randy said, "I've been at Belmont for ten years now."

I laughed, saying, "More like six months, Randy, not ten years."

"No wonder I'm crazy, I've been getting a lot done. In a certain way, Belmont has been nice. I wouldn't call it home, though. Home is where Mom and Dad are in Laguna Beach."

"Yeah," I agreed. "I miss them, Randy. I miss Mom especially."

"Mom?" he said. "Mom and Dad are still around, Diane. I know 'cause I talked to them a couple of days ago. I talked to one, then the other, but I didn't talk to them in unison."

One of my favorite excursions led us to Valhalla Memorial Park Cemetery, a broken-down resting place to thousands of deceased residents. Wandering through a sea of headstones illustrating photographs of the departed, I couldn't help but compare it with the National Cemetery in San Francisco, where a sea of white crosses frames the great Pacific Ocean. As we sat on a concrete bench under a drooping oak tree, Randy began a description of an encounter with Brenda, the friendly, unassuming receptionist at Belmont Village.

"Are you ready for this one, Diane? It's unbelievable. One day, Brenda and I walked into this empty room, and she did something that utterly amazed me. Remember, now, this was

Brenda. Anyway, she said, 'Randy, do you wanna dance?' I said, 'Sure.' So I put my arm around her and we started dancing. There was no music, so I started humming a very pretty song. For the life of me, I can't think of it now. Anyway, we danced for four or five minutes. When it was over, she looked at me and said, 'I think I love you.' The next day, she greeted me at the front desk with 'Hi, kiddo.' The romance was off. The following week, she asked me if I wanted to dance again. I think that's why she fascinates me. She's truly a puzzle. Now, here's the tricky part. . . . Brenda doesn't want me to get near Miriam. As Miriam, Brenda is more matter of fact. She's Miriam. She's not some dreamer like Brenda. Can you believe it? They are exactly the same person."

Not knowing exactly how to respond, I said, "What a great story, Randy. So detailed." I got up and walked over to get a closer look at an etched granite headstone incorporating a black-and-white photograph of a dark-haired boy with a big smile who had died on July 17, 2005, at the age of seven. It made me think of little Randy's constant blank-faced smile. As I looked up to see him lumbering toward the broken-down mausoleum, I thought about the insane story he had so flawlessly woven. Did it mean that having dementia opened up new vistas, new perceptions? Randy had never been more content. He'd never been more affectionate, available, and even vulnerable. Was it that he finally felt free to live with people, to be instinctively aware of how lucky he was to have a "Hillary" in his life? But I did know one thing for certain—that for the first time in a long time I looked forward to seeing Randy. I even began to anticipate the weekend visits and what surprises

Randy would share with that inimitable mind of his. Our unexpected bond began to grow. Perhaps his highly inventive, newly scattered brain enriched his ability to share feelings and thoughts without impulsively erecting walls that protected him from people.

One Sunday, about a year after Randy had arrived at Belmont, I took the elevator to his third-floor apartment and knocked on the door. Once inside, I noticed that all the collages had been taken off the walls. "Yeah, I took them down. I don't see myself as a great artist. You know what I want? I want to be part of the unexpected surprise. If I were to take a photograph of a person, I'd want to catch that person out of character. That doesn't mean looking goofy. It means I'd want to catch him or her when he or she is not being who they pretend they are. I'd like to grasp—'grasp' is the right word, right?—anyway, I'd like to be a witness to their unseen beauty."

This time, our drive took us to my friends Josh Schweitzer and Mary Sue Milliken's house for dinner. When we arrived, Randy seemed distracted. Josh shook his hand and ushered him in, but Randy looked puzzled. "I can't remember your name," he said. "I hope you don't mind. What is it again?" Later, when Duke and I were talking to him, he said, "That's your son?" He hadn't recognized him. After dinner, he told me he was uncomfortable because he couldn't keep up with the conversation. He was beginning to lose the battle with memory in an all-too-familiar way.

In 2014, at the end of his third year at Belmont, a letter from Hillary told us what was already becoming clear: this golden period for Randy was coming to an end.

Dear Diane, Robin and Dorrie,

In a lot of ways Randy continues to try to rediscover himself, while also losing himself all over again. His past is beginning to catch up with him. As you all know, this last year Randy's slowed down, and so have our adventures. He forgets where we've been by the next visit. He continues to look at his writing as a job. He still puts pen to paper, sometimes staying up all night, or walking early in the morning. He thinks he'd go crazy if he couldn't write. He loves his table and the street below with the light coming through his window making crazy shadows in the room. Cutting out magazines, writing, listening to music, and eating dry cereal with honey and oats makes him happy.

As his memory fades, he started doing strange things, like putting Vitamin Water in his coffee because it makes it sweet. Sometimes he has the heat so high it feels like a sauna in his room. Sometimes he answers the door naked. Things are becoming more of a crap shoot. What will I find as I walk into this room?

I continue to write on his calendar to try and help him keep track of time, but somehow the calendars have started to disappear. I have to take him for an outing, or to get lunch, so the staff at Belmont have enough time to come in and vacuum, change the sheets and towels and clean the bathroom. It is absolute hell if we come back to someone in his room. He's been observed by the staff getting extremely frustrated and upset if even the slightest thing is wrong. For example, he was reading a play and couldn't follow where the characters were or what they were conveying. He became very agitated. Another time he was playing a game that involved little tile pieces. He had to put down a 5 but he couldn't find it, even though it was right in front of his face. He was so mad he threw the tiles across the table, got up and stormed off. He hides things. He hoards them, too. He hides his money because he's afraid someone will take it, and then gets horribly upset when he can't find it. He won't let me throw away his old coffee bags because he might use them in a collage. These are difficult days.

All the best, Hillary

CHAPTER 14

KICKED OUT

Two major events secured Randy's removal from Belmont in 2015. One morning, he fell out of bed, hit his head, and was rushed to the USC Medical Center, where he was put in a medically induced coma. The doctors determined he'd had a stroke. Once he returned, he began lashing out at people, even Hillary. He kicked trash cans, threw chairs, hit walls. His anger was back, full-force. There was no explanation. Hillary and I took him to a highly recommended psychiatrist in Westwood, who suggested we arrange a physical examination. The results revealed signs of advanced dementia, as evidenced by rigid muscles, tremors, trouble with balance, and even hallucinations. And so to his list of woes was added, above all, Parkinson's disease.

A few weeks later, Hillary called and said that Randy was in a rage. He wanted out of Belmont and was freaked about his keys. Someone had stolen them—not once, but twice, maybe three times, actually. The next morning, she opened the door to punched-out walls, collages flung all over the floor. Hoping to escape from his fury, Hillary decided to take him to see one of my movies. When they came back to Belmont, he got all riled up about the keys again. He started screaming. Hillary found them inside a door hinge. She also opened a drawer and found a half-eaten yogurt, collecting mold, next to important meds, Aricept, which was supposed to help with his dementia symptoms, and Seroquel, for his bipolar disorder. Because he hadn't been taking his medications, Randy's week had been horrific.

It was then that Dorrie and I were politely informed that Randy's impulsivity had forced the staff to request his departure from Belmont. Perhaps he needed the kind of care provided by a convalescent home. The place they recommended was out of the question for me. Hillary lived in L.A., and so did I. We started looking for something closer. Sunrise Villa Senior Living, for older adults who value their independence but need some assistance with daily activities, was located in Culver City. After Hillary and I took a tour of the Spanish Revival facility, we agreed this would become Randy's new home.

As Hillary and I began packing up Randy's belongings, something strange happened. Dorrie called from the 405 Freeway in Valencia, and she was shouting into the phone. "Diane! Listen to me. I just turned away from looking at Six Flags' world-record nineteen roller coasters when, I swear to God, I spotted a random office building with a large gray sign on top spelling out the words Hall and Foreman. Can you believe it? Dad's old company sign in Valencia? Can you believe it?"

"Slow down, Dorr. How could there possibly be a Hall and Foreman sign, much less one on top of an office building across the street from Magic Mountain? There is no more Hall and Foreman. Not possible."

"Diane, I'm telling you it's true." And with that she started crying. I listened to her sob into the phone, with the sound of cars behind her, until she was ready to hang up.

The very next day, I drove to Valencia and looked across the freeway from Six Flags. Sure enough, there, on a frontage road lined with office buildings, stood a seven-foot-high sign with letters spelling out our father's company's name. Like Dorrie before me, I burst into tears. Jack Newton Ignatius Hall—Mary Hall's son, Dorothy's husband of forty-six years, our father, USC graduate, civil engineer, president of Hall and Foreman, "breadwinner"—had returned in the form of a seven-foot-high gray sign in bold white letters. I took one last look at Dad's sign, picked up my iPhone, and called the owner of the building. When his assistant put him on, I asked if he was interested in selling the sign. As of one month later, Hall and Foreman stands in my rented warehouse, waiting for me to step up and buy the horse ranch across the street from Mom and Dad's old Tubac, Arizona, home, which Dorrie owns. What a tribute that would be . . . right there where their ashes rest under a variety of crosses.

A few weeks later, Dorrie joined Hillary and me in packing to move to Sunrise. I came across one of Mom's old eight-by-ten-inch portraits. Randy has to be in his early twenties. His hair is greasy, and he's beginning to gain weight. His full body sits in profile on one of those cheap scalloped Mexican chairs we must have bought in Tijuana. He looks down at a piece of paper in his hands. Mom's photograph has not aged well. As for Randy, I can see he's beginning his long journey into isolation. Superimposed over his body by Mom in collage form is a poem he wrote, "the study of birds' eggs."

The ribbon on Mom's typewriter must have been running out of ink, because quite a few letters have disappeared and others inexplicably stand out. Who knows, perhaps she was thinking of clever ways to seduce editors at literary journals like *Granta* and *The Kenyon Review* with an intriguing mystery.

It's hard to believe Randy wrote:

A delicate hand is preferred for reasons obvious to anyone with eggs in mind. The fingers must be narrow, soft and able to fit through small openings in all but the younger trees, because when all's said and done, a closed fist in the Lab isn't worth an egg in the pan. With steady nerve and careful transport, the label V for various markings of the dodo, dove, and duck is just the beginning of the hard part. Each bird egg is individually wrapped in a felt jacket and sent to x-ray for proof of age and estimated release. If there is the slightest scratch the egg is sent back to its mother and she decides in what fashion it must be raised. This brings out the woman in all of us, and the sudden urge to nurse anything made of porcelain becomes painful and downright obscene.

Why did Mom type this poem and place it here? I can't begin to imagine what she was thinking when she transcribed the bizarre reference to being raised by a woman who needs to nurse anything made of porcelain, a process not only painful but also "obscene." She couldn't possibly have thought this was one of Randy's engaging page-turners. Was it a reference to his hypersensitivity and abandonment? Layering such a bizarre statement over a photograph of her son staring down into what must have been the poem itself, if it was a poem—who was going to be the audience of this ill-defined project? No one. Only me. And only fifty years later.

The two of them, Mom and Randy, were "the Almost Artists." Randy didn't have to follow the rules and learn. He took his form of expression, collage and poetry, to the limits of his ability. No matter how misguided he became, Mom flew to him without question, celebrating what he described as his *"mad gathering of words in an attempt to explain black wishes set against the earth's silence."*

CHAPTER 15

LET IT GO

After Randy settled into Sunrise Villa, he began knocking on the neighbors' doors. Imagine their surprise to find a tall, elderly man with a white beard. After "Hello," and "Can we help you with anything?," Randy asked them if they would mind driving him to his mom and dad's house at 905 North Wright Street in Santa Ana. He needed to go home. Despite being turned down several times, Randy continued knocking on several other doors, until the police arrived and took him across the street to his new, real home.

Now deemed a risk, Randy seemed to be repeating patterns that created the same problems he had had in Laguna when the police were called. It was like he wanted to be given a chance to go back to Mom and Dad, to find a way into a safe world that removed him from responsibility. Some things never change.

The next day, Randy was taken out of his community suite and moved into a studio apartment on the first floor of the "Memory Care" wing at Sunrise. According to Sunrise's brochure, each resident in their Memory Care program has a "life enrichment manager." All tenants have access to everything, with the notable exception of both entrance and exit doors, which feature keypads with secret code numbers to prevent independent strolls outside the perimeters of the kindly detention center for seniors with Alzheimer's disease and other forms of dementia. There are no views from inside the seven-thousand-square-foot walled-off living quarters. Most travel takes place within the six-foot-wide corridor. Randy's fellow residents John and William must have put in a few miles the day he passed them to enter his new one-room apartment. A former Air Force pilot turned stockbroker, John didn't cotton to people. As for William, when he wasn't walking the halls, he liked to sit next to female residents and stare at them for hours.

Randy's first night in Memory Care was noteworthy. At 1:00 a.m., he took the liberty of exploring bald-headed Bob's room. Once inside, he removed his clothes and defecated in Bob's trash can. Completely naked, he proceeded to the next room, pulled down the sheets, and got into bed with eighty-one-year-old Lillian, who woke up screaming bloody murder. Lillian, a former bookkeeper from Boston, rarely spoke, much less screamed. Residents didn't talk much unless they were spoken to. When one of the staff members asked Randy what the heck he thought he was doing in her bed, Randy claimed he had to get Hillary's car keys, because he was going to drive to his mom and dad's house in Santa Ana.

. . .

began visiting Randy and his new friends every weekend. On our way to lunch in the dining room that first Saturday, we passed wheelchair-bound fifty-seven-year-old Mark, an entertainment lawyer who prematurely wound up in Memory Care after several strokes affected his ability to walk. Frisky Monty, a former race-car driver, had short-term memory loss. One of her twin boys fell off a rooftop and died at fifteen. She never recovered from his demise. Everyone agreed that Elizabeth Taylor's alleged former seamstress, Eleanora, was a "tiny pistol" ready to explode; one staff member quit because she repeatedly tried to attack him. As petite as Eleanora was, she'd consume three helpings of food at a sitting, and always with her hands. If she didn't like what was on offer, she tossed the entire plate across the room. If someone gave her the wrong juice, she'd throw it at them. It took three caregivers to shower her. After several months, she was politely escorted out of Memory Care.

Sitting in Randy's room with his weekend caregiver, Delia, I was surprised by Randy's insights on Eleanora. "I try to steer clear of Eleanora, because I find her an abstraction. But, today, she struck me as informed, for a change. Someone said she caused people to say weird things. I don't understand the big hoopla. They're dead wrong. What she does is cause people to think. Eleanora's someone I would like to write about in the future."

Suddenly Smitty walked into Randy's room, enraged. He didn't belong in this zoo. He'd been falsely diagnosed with a so-called serious case of Alzheimer's, which, he said, was on the brink of being cleared up in a matter of weeks.

The Memory Care residents were much more entertaining than the "Independent Living" seniors on the other side of lockdown. One could say that Randy and his new friends were on the losing side of life, but the truth was, they shared a unique capacity to respond in the moment without fear of consequences. The "Independents" seemed stuck in a routine that boxed out extemporaneous behavior.

After six months, Steve, the new occupational therapist, Delia, and I were walking Randy around the hallway when he suddenly blurted out, "Don't talk, 'cause I'm swimming." When he had blown out the candles on his sixty-ninth birthday, Randy paused to make this announcement: "Sometimes I forget. Sometimes I'm really confused. I remember my girlfriend wandered off. It was inevitable. It just didn't work. It wasn't meant to happen. Remember Sally? She used to live in San Diego. Now she lives in the expensive area. I don't begrudge her anything." I didn't have the heart to tell him that his ex-wife, Sally, had died in 2006 after a botched surgical procedure.

One Sunday, in an effort to capture Randy's attention, I brought in my black-velvet-covered photography book, *The Plot Thickens,* in which a host of master photographers present the opportunity to look and think about the art of photography in this cell-phone age, "when paying attention may become a disappearing art." When I pointed out an August Sander photograph of an eye staring into the camera lens, he couldn't get over it. "I like this one because the eye got created by a bird building her nest. That's where the eggs are laid, in nests, right?" For a moment he paused, then looked at me. "I don't know if I've accomplished what I wanted in life. I think

I've challenged people. But there have been some I couldn't put a dent in even if I took an atom bomb and stuck it in their ear."

Soon after, Randy stopped mentioning collages or poems. His hands shook more predominantly. He no longer joined the other residents to cut and paste art projects with glue and crayons. He stopped writing words on paper.

In the fall, we sat down in the lounge and watched *Gone with the Wind* in a room full of mostly sleeping friends. At a certain point, I asked Randy if he thought Vivien Leigh and Clark Gable had been acting out something more moving than the words in the script. Did he think they were using their own life experiences, perhaps even their longing for a love they couldn't allow themselves to feel in real life? Randy looked at me like I was crazy.

Smitty, sitting next to him, looked my way and started in with "Why are you wearing a hat? You look like an ugly old man. Get out of here."

Before returning to the wonder of Rhett Butler riding away from the wreckage of Tara, Randy said, "I keep forgetting that when I die there will no longer be live television."

"Good point, Randy. Good point," I said.

I've heard that if you keep a parakeet in a cage for years and you take it out, it will die. I guess sometimes the best idea is to stay in the cage. Randy did. I've also heard that once you've spent a life in solitary confinement you've lost a part of who you are. Curiously, it was this kind of social death, combined with being excluded from society and all of its rules and expectations, that Randy sought out. Looking at it from a distance, you could say his near-total isolation exacted a terrible price. And yet it also had a certain value.

Revisiting Randy's past feels like an investigation composed of hundreds of clues, often leading nowhere. The new version of an old story doesn't assure validity, but the reality of the present does. While visiting Randy in lockdown, I couldn't help being engaged by the fact that life is inexplicable, in myriad ways. No one can predict who is going to touch your heart in a way that changes your very being. And there are no concrete answers to why any of us are the way we are. Randy was a mystery. But so was I. So were Mom and Dad. Would Randy have had such fantasies if he hadn't had a mother who worshipped him? And would he have been obsessed with making collages from torn paper and found objects if he hadn't had a father who insisted he go to Toastmasters until the age of twenty-three? Would it have made a difference? There are no answers.

Time passes. Week by week, day by day, and moment by moment, Randy began to use one less word in a sentence. Eventually, he was down to "Yes," "Right," and "No." Six months earlier he'd said, "It's getting tough, this age stuff. I'm sixty-three or sixty-four."

"You're sixty-nine," I reminded him.

"Am I really? That doesn't scare me. . . . Sixty-nine, huh? Okay. Sixty-nine. What am I going to do about it, cut off a finger now that I'm sixty-nine?"

Full sentences were a deeply appreciated, rare form of

communication. Soon, I began to take the liberty of holding Randy's long fingers in my hands. I'd kiss his forehead, or touch his white hair, and pinch his cheeks. After a lifetime of self-imposed barriers, I finally gave myself permission to be close, quiet, and intimate with my brother.

CHAPTER 16

HOMEWARD BOUND

I'd taken a few days off to visit Dorrie in New Mexico. She picked me up at the train station in Lamy, a small town just outside of Santa Fe, and we enjoyed a few easy days together. She'd sold a rare cast-iron rabbit ashtray stand by Thomas Molesworth, and, even better, her high-end Monterey club chair went for more than she expected at the yearly Objects of Art show held at Santa Fe's El Museo Cultural. She was feeling good. In celebration, we shared a drink on the rooftop of the La Fonda Hotel and watched the evening clouds gather as in a Maynard Dixon landscape. It had been a dream trip. While Dorrie sold, I'd walked around the plaza, hit the galleries, and visited the Georgia O'Keeffe Museum, where I was taken with her painting *Patio Door with Green Leaf*.

When it's time to go back to L.A., Dorrie drops me off in Lamy, at the train station. After waiting an interminably long amount of time for Amtrak's Southwest Chief to arrive, I go for a walk along an abandoned railroad track, which leads to an old

Pullman sleeping car resting in front of a nineteenth-century adobe chapel with a bell tower. Lamy, population 219, would be right up Randy's alley. I begin to envision an extended family, maybe ours, living peacefully there. We'd have to include Delia with her new dog, Elvis, and Hillary plus her sons, Dylan and Owen. Of course, Robin would join us with her husband, Rickey, her daughter, Riley, and son, Jack. Dorrie would arrive with her two dogs, Milo and Willa, but also her Monterey furniture, Western paintings, road signs, and her rare collection of Indian jewelry. I'd greet them all, accompanied by Duke, Dexter, and Emmie, our fourteen-year-old dog.

After he acclimated to a rural life in our new digs, Randy could sit in his wheelchair as Hillary or Delia, or I, pushed him past the historic plaque in Lamy's park, the one I know he'd never get tired of reading: "In March of 1880 one of the locals sighted a fish-shaped balloon which contained ten human occupants singing and shouting in an unknown language. A large red rose was reportedly dropped from the floating dirigible."

As the train finally pulls into the station, I resist picking up my luggage. But life at home calls. Reluctantly, I roll my black suitcase toward the tracks.

Once inside, I let go of yearning for a future that can't be realized, sit down, pick up the Southwest Chief Route Guide to read about our first stop, Albuquerque, New Mexico. Since 1946, the year I was born, it had been home to Sandia Base, at the time the United States' principal nuclear-weapons installation. Atomic bombs were developed and tested in secret within its perimeters. Sandia bore the responsibility of keeping the country's covert military operations safe from danger. I can't help but think of Randy and how he kept his fantasies hidden in spiral notebooks, also safe from danger. In them he scrutinized fantasies of revenge, but also the mystery of love.

It's pitch-black as we pass Flagstaff, Arizona, home to the Lowell Observatory. In 1958, the city passed the nation's first ordinance governing outdoor lighting in order to preserve its dark skies. Dark skies used to terrify little Randy. The sheer vastness of night was a problem he couldn't solve. What if he fell into the darkness and disappeared forever and ever? These days, his eyes are full of unapproachable thoughts. It's as if he's living the effects of a waking dream.

What a contrast to fat Randy at Belmont, smiling into my camera lens with two missing teeth. I ask myself if my early disdain for his ever-ready smile was based on the fact that I copied it. Even in his darkest days, he wore it to great effect.

At least Randy's gift was not mean-spirited. For some people, harmlessness is all they have to offer. My brother and I have done a good job selling our brand of the innocuous encounter. I'm well aware I've made a career out of it. Behind those countless hellos, those challenging yet friendly dinner conversations filled with struggling attempts to join in, behind all that, Randy and I succeeded in arming ourselves against the vicissitudes of intimacy.

Percival Lowell, the descendant of a Boston Brahmin family, established his observatory in 1894 to study the possibility of intelligent life on Mars. The observatory's astronomers made discoveries that altered our understanding of space, including Clyde Tombaugh's discovery of Pluto in 1930.

Dad made a discovery the day I walked with him along Le Conte Avenue to the UCLA Medical Center, where he was going to get his radiation treatment. He wasn't in a hurry. Not anymore. At one point, he bent down, picked up a cigar band in the gutter, and gave it to me. He then wandered off and stopped to look at a cluster of crows in an old eucalyptus tree. I tried to engage him with the new ring, but Dad was having none of it—he was looking at the crows. Though known for their intelligence, the shiny black birds are considered bad luck and even harbingers of death, yet some say the presence of a dead crow means the end of bad times, and the beginning of good.

In decline, both father and son became seekers of the absurd. Afflicted with a brain tumor that would kill him in just a few months, Dad said from his seaside bedroom, "You know, Dot, it looks like I'll be taking over the Ronald Reagan job for Northrop soon. Hey, you know what's interesting about perspective? See the top of the glass there? Let's assume the top of the glass creates a perspective with an illusion created by another line. Oh, and, Dorothy, you missed something last night. Fergit Fillman, Frog's father, was here. I told him Dorrie and Randy were coming on Sunday. I want to see their joyous faces when they dance around the lobby."

A friendly Amtrak attendant knocks on my door and announces that breakfast is being served as the train arrives in Riverside, California. Having read my Southwest Chief

Route Guide, I know that in the late nineteenth century a certain Eliza Tibbets received two orange trees from a friend and planted them in Riverside, where they thrived. I remember Randy and me sneaking into the Rohrses vast grove to steal as many oranges as we could. We'd hide them in our pockets so we wouldn't get caught. As time went on, we became witnesses to the grove's gradual disappearance. When the last tree was finally chopped down, all that was left was a twenty-five-acre mound of dirt.

Like Marie Rohrs's old orange grove, Randy is disappearing. The inevitable truth of goodbye fills me with remorse and also guilt. If only I could find one paragraph in Mom's journals that describes me as helping him out with his ABCs, or letting him go before me to sit on Santa Claus's lap. If only I could find one photograph in the dozens of Hall family scrapbooks that documented me patting him on the back for a job well done or, I don't know, giving him my very own box of See's candy as a gesture of kindness. Did I ever crawl down the ladder from the top of our bunk bed at night and help him brave the dark he was so frightened of? If only.

Before my brother slammed his fist through a wall; before he tried to commit suicide by gassing himself inside his Volkswagen van in the garage of his Tangerine Street town house; before he threw Dorrie and me out of Carol Kane's cottage— before, but also after, he's been what many would call a crazy brother. Yes, his mind has always been his torture, but also his treasure. And mine. I just wish I'd seen it sooner.

Like the sparrows, hummingbirds, and blue jays who flew into our glass windows, Randy has had his share of catastrophes. Birds spoke to him; their flight soothed his way. Maybe he was thanking them when he wrote:

I've always been the never-ready boy, the stunted boy. Slow to catch on to the world and the people in it. It took time to find out where I belonged. The simple answer is . . . nowhere. This morning, in front of my window, seabirds glide. Their feathered bodies lay grace to shame. I watch and think how clumsy I am; how my abilities do not suit me. I've spent a life nesting on fear and regret. I am not an airborne soul. I never once reached for what is just beyond my window.

Outside the train window, the sky is framed by the Riverside Mountains. So beautiful. I am coming to accept that these are the let-it-go days. The days of getting my will in order. I will leave Duke the Bob Boltz six-by-five-foot car-crash photograph as a reminder to be cautious while driving. Dexter will receive Cindy Sherman's self-portrait of a woman unhinged, so she can learn to stay calm when things go askew. Mom left me her Pottery Barn table. It sat in a warehouse until, one day, I finally let it go. I want that Pottery Barn table back. I want Randy back, too. I want to have another chance at being a better sister.

The train surges forward. I start singing an old Irving Berlin song Mom used to play on the piano: "How much do I love you? I'll tell you no lie. How deep is the ocean? How high is the sky? . . . And if I ever lost you, how much would I cry? How deep is the ocean? How high is the sky?"

ACKNOWLEDGMENTS

Robin Desser, *whose brilliance guided the path all the way to the finish line*

Annie Bishai

Dorrie Hall

Robin Bevington

Jean Heaton

Stephanie Heaton

Sarah Rothbard

Hillary McFarland

Delia Jimenez

Steve Barbour

Dr. Gary Pevnick

Cherry on Top Frozen Yogurt

Marilyn Anderson

Roya Robati

Simon Toop

Lilly Sandberg

Kristen Wolf

Erinn Hartman

Demetris Papadimitropoulos

Lydia Buechler

Soonyoung Kwon

John Gall

Daniel Novack

Roméo Enriquez

Andy Hughes

Paul Bogaards

ILLUSTRATIONS

All photos courtesy of Diane Keaton

Diane Keaton has starred in some of the most memorable films of the past forty years, including the *Godfather* trilogy, *Annie Hall, Manhattan, Reds, Baby Boom, The First Wives Club,* and *Something's Gotta Give.* Her many awards include the Golden Globe and the Academy Award. She is the author of the *New York Times* best-selling memoir *Then Again* and the essay collection *Let's Just Say It Wasn't Pretty.* Keaton lives with her daughter and son in Los Angeles.

A NOTE ON THE TYPE

This book was set in a version of the well-known Monotype face Bembo. This letter was cut for the celebrated Venetian printer Aldus Manutius by Francesco Griffo, and first used in Pietro Cardinal Bembo's *De Aetna* of 1495. The companion italic is an adaptation of the chancery script type designed by the calligrapher and printer Lodovico degli Arrighi.

Composed by North Market Street Graphics,
Lancaster, Pennsylvania

Printed and bound by Berryville Graphics,
Berryville, Virginia

Designed by Soonyoung Kwon